WITHDRAWN

EASY LAWNS

Low Maintenance

Native Grasses

For Gardeners

Everywhere

Stevie Daniels-Guest Editor

Janet Marinelli

SERIES EDITOR

Jane Ludlam

MANAGING EDITOR

Bekka Lindstrom

ART DIRECTOR

Mark Tebbitt

SCIENCE EDITOR

Handbook #160

Copyright © Fall 1999 by the Brooklyn Botanic Garden, Inc.

Handbooks in the *21st-Century Gardening Series,* formerly *Plants & Gardens,*
are published quarterly at 1000 Washington Ave., Brooklyn, NY 11225.

Subscription included in Brooklyn Botanic Garden subscriber membership dues ($45.00 per year).

ISSN # 0362-5850   ISBN # 1-889538-12-4

Printed by Science Press, a division of the Mack Printing Group, on recycled paper.

Cover photograph: Buffalograss '609' in Texas

• TABLE OF CONTENTS •

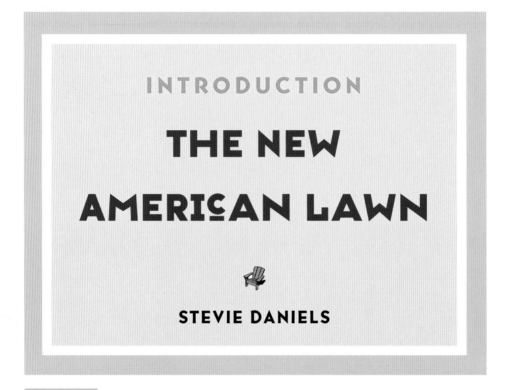

INTRODUCTION

THE NEW AMERICAN LAWN

STEVIE DANIELS

FIFTEEN YEARS AGO environmental concerns spurred the movement to reduce the size of the lawn or replace it with other plants. Back then, even in Colorado, parts of the Southwest, and California, where annual rainfall is 15 inches or less, turfgrasses native to Eurasia and adapted to double that amount of precipitation were considered the ideal. This practice put an unnecessary strain on limited water resources. Synthetic fertilizers and pesticides used to keep the grass green and weed-free were degrading water quality and harming nontarget animals and plants.

As a result of these concerns, interest has grown in alternatives to the conventional lawn, including the use of native plants in more naturalistic landscape designs, xeriscaping or low-water landscaping, creating backyard wildlife habitat, planting wildflowers in home gardens and roadside plantings, replacing lawns with groundcovers, and restoring native plant communities. Meadow and prairie plantings have been popular and logical substitutes for lawns. Another strategy has been to take a more relaxed approach to lawn care: not fertilizing or controlling weeds, just mowing whatever grows.

A buffalograss lawn in New Braunfels, Texas, is both beautiful and carefree.

As I've traveled around the country exploring the landscapes of home-owners who've been growing native plants and establishing meadows or prairies, I've discovered that while many people want an alternative to their water- and chemical-dependent lawn, they don't always want a three-foot meadow. They still want a low-growing grassy area where children can play, or they can relax and entertain. I began to wonder, why have we become tied to using only nonnative species that need to be coddled with regular infusions of fertilizer, pesticides, and water? Why can't native grasses, which are better adapted to particular locales, be used in place of the imported turfgrasses? Why have we become mesmerized by the idea that a lawn has to look like a closely cropped green carpet?

I began replacing the lawn in my own yard with blends of native grass-es, and I talked with native-grass experts about my idea. I discovered there are suitable grass species adapted to particular regions of the coun-try. I also learned that this country has hundreds of locally adapted sedges (grasslike plants) that also can be used in place of a lawn.

The leading experts on native grasses and sedges have written chap-ters for this book. Five of the chapters that follow focus on specific grass or sedge varieties suitable for use across a wide geographic range. Another six chapters are written by either nursery owners or horticulturists from specific regions; they focus on the native grasses that are best suited to their areas and how to grow them. Still another chapter provides simple, step-by-step instructions on how to get your native grass lawn started. At the end of the book, you'll find profiles of the best native lawn grasses for every region, as well as a comprehensive list of seed suppliers.

GOING NATIVE

In the United States, 1,400 species of 170 genera of grass are indigenous. Of the 14 species that the Lawn Institute claims are suitable for turf, only two are native—buffalograss (*Buchloë dactyloides*), and red fescue (*Festuca rubra*). The typical lawngrasses—from Kentucky bluegrass (*Poa pratensis*) to bermudagrass (*Cynodon dactylon*)—are not native.

The best example of a native grass being used for lawn—a great success story—is buffalograss. Native throughout the Great Plains, from Minnesota to Montana and south into Mexico, it grows where the soil is not too moist, too dry, or too shady. It can handle –30°F and high heat. It has a fine, soft texture and spreads by stolons that root at the nodes or joints. Slow growing, it reaches a height of only 6 inches. Unlike most nonnative turfgrasses, buffalograss needs minimal water once established and no fertilizer. The first buffalograss cultivars bred specifically for lawn use were developed in the early 1990s by M. C. Engelke and his student (at the time), Virginia Lehman, of Texas A&M Experiment Station in Dallas, and Terrance P. Riordan, of the University of Nebraska (author of "Planting and Maintaining a Buffalograss Lawn," page 16).

Turfgrass researchers have also worked to improve fine fescues, a group that includes red, hard, and sheep fescue. These grasses are also slow growing, reaching a height of 8 inches. They can handle dry soil and extreme cold. They can take the heat of the upper South but do not do well in the extreme heat and humidity of the deep South. Until now, the new cultivars of these grasses have been considered a minor component in turfgrass blends that still contain mostly Kentucky bluegrass. In this book, you'll learn how to use them alone or with other native grasses.

Choosing a native grass or group of grasses suited to a particular locale is the way to create a true "natural" lawn. It doesn't have to be a 3-foot-high meadow—the grasses and sedges you will read about in this book give you the opportunity to have a lawnlike planting of indigenous species while eliminating the need to apply fertilizer regularly, mow

In places where a formal look is not necessary, a meadow of native grasses and wildflowers is a beautiful replacement for a lawn.

every week, and use herbicides.

An additional benefit is that you will be restoring the native sod found in open sunny areas before agriculture and development transformed regional American landscapes. Lawns of nonnative species interrupt the natural landscape, breaking up the continuum of native habitats and contributing to the loss of biodiversity.

In some cases, you actually will be helping to prevent the disappearance of important forage and habitat grasses. For instance, junegrass (*Koeleria macrantha*) once grew widely across Pennsylvania, but due to agriculture, urban development, and the reversion of open areas back to forest, it is rare to find it now. In Florida, wiregrass and pinewoods dropseed at one time covered more than 50 percent of the state. Now they are found only in small preserves. Meanwhile, homeowners across that state struggle with irrigation systems, pests, and diseases while trying to maintain St. Augustinegrass, bahiagrass, or zoysia.

A number of the native species suitable for use in a lawnlike planting are naturally low growing (5 to 6 inches), which means they can be left

ESSENTIAL TERMS

COOL-SEASON GRASS: A grass that grows best in spring and fall, blooms and sets seed in late spring or early summer, grows slowly or goes dormant in summer, greens up again in fall, and stays green into winter.

WARM-SEASON GRASS: A grass that does most of its growing in the hot summer, blooms and sets seed in the fall, and goes dormant when cold whether arrives.

BUNCHGRASS: A grass that grows in a circular clump that gets larger each year. Because bunchgrasses do not spread and fill in thickly, they need to be seeded at a higher rate than sod-forming grasses for a thick stand of lawn.

SOD-FORMING GRASS: A grass that sends out stolons (stems that grow along the soil surface and root at the joints) or rhizomes (underground stems that root and send up new plants away from the original plant) and therefore tends to spread and fill in thickly.

BULK SEED: Seed with chaff (anything that's not seed) mixed in.

PURE LIVE SEED (PLS): Seed from which chaff has been removed. When ordering native grass seed, it is a good idea to specify your needs in PLS. Most recommended seeding rates are listed as PLS.

FORB: A broad-leaved herbaceous plant that grows alongside grasses in a field, prairie, meadow, or lawn.

unmowed if desired. Others grow somewhat taller and send up attractive seed-bearing stems. For homeowners who prefer a smoother appearance, both the short and tall types can be cut once or twice during the growing season. Since you will be creating habitat for small mammals, ground-nesting birds, and other wildlife, it is important to avoid cutting during nesting times; thus, very early spring or late fall are the best times to mow.

Native grasses, like nonnatives, can be divided into two main groups based on their growing habits: cool-season grasses, those that grow best in spring and fall, bloom and set seed in late spring or early summer, grow slowly or go dormant in summer, and stay green into winter; and warm-season, those that do most of their growing in the hot summer, bloom and set seed in the fall, and turn beige or other interesting colors when cold weather arrives. You can try blending a warm-season and a cool-season grass to extend the time the planting looks green, although the result might be a little uneven, depending on which grass dominates in a particular spot.

Another characteristic of grasses that will help you understand how to grow and manage them is growth habit. The two main types are bunch

Unlike conventional turf, native grasses and wildflowers provide wildlife habitat. Here, a sphinx moth probes for nectar in a beebalm flower.

and spreading (or sod-forming). A bunchgrass grows in a circular clump, getting larger each year. Spreading grasses send out stolons (stems that grow along the soil surface and root at the joints) or rhizomes (underground stems that root and send up new plants away from the original plant). Most warm-season grasses are bunch types. They do not spread and fill in thickly as does a sod-forming or rhizomatous grass. Because they don't fill in thickly, you will need to sow seed at a higher rate to prevent broadleaf weeds from getting established, or you can use the opportunity to interplant low-growing wildflowers.

Another important thing to understand is why turfgrass is usually sold in mixtures. The goal is to plant the blend of grasses best suited to a site that will fill in thickly to keep weeds out. The blend ideally includes species that germinate quickly and cover the ground to give slower ones time to get started, species that are adapted to dry spots, others adapted to wet areas, and some that can tolerate light shade. The same should be true of native turfgrass mixtures. If you plant little bluestem and blue grama, the little bluestem will migrate to moister areas and the blue grama to drier areas.

Your satisfaction with a native lawn may depend on accepting a new aesthetic.
Unmowed native grasses such as sideoats grama reflect the beauty of natural meadows.

A NEW LAWN AESTHETIC

Like any natural landscape, a native lawn is not created by a "just let it go" approach. Nor is it inexpensive. You can expect to pay the same or slightly more than you would to install a new conventional lawn. A native lawn also requires just as much care in selecting the plant mix. The difference is you will be creating a landscape that is sustainable. Once established, a native lawn will require vastly less maintenance than a conventional lawn. If you desire a perfectly manicured lawn, you might want to weigh that desire with the costs to keep it that way.

The information about using native grasses and sedges for lawns is new and still evolving. This book is the first to provide guidance for regions throughout the country. Some of you who try it will be pioneering, especially if you experiment with blends of species or choose a grass that is native to your area but has not been tried in a lawn planting.

To some extent, your satisfaction will depend on accepting an aesthetic based on the beauty of your natural landscape. Look at open meadows in natural settings—that's the vision toward which we are moving.

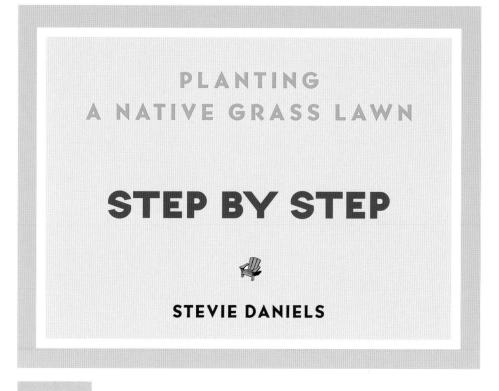

PLANTING
A NATIVE GRASS LAWN

STEP BY STEP

STEVIE DANIELS

FOLLOW THESE BASIC STEPS to plant a lawn of native grasses no matter where you live. For more directions that are specific to your area, see the chapters on regional approaches to planting a native lawn. For instance, "Native Grasses for High Desert Landscapes" covers watering during the first year of establishment in the Southwest. For more information on the planting requirements of a particular species, refer to the chapters on specific grasses, such as "Planting and Maintaining Buffalograss."

Warm-season grasses need a soil temperature of at least 60°F to germinate, so the best time to plant is late spring or early summer. Cool-season grasses germinate best in fall.

SELECT THE SITE. All of the grasses need full sun and a well-drained soil. The sedges (see "Sedge Lawns for Every Landscape," page 31), and some of the fine fescues (see "Low & Slow Fescues," page 26) will tolerate partial shade. Measure the site to determine the number of square feet.

Step 3: A tiller will help clear the site.

2 BUY THE SEED OR PLUGS. Seed is available year-round, but it is best to place your order early (in December or January), since suppliers run out of certain varieties. Plugs are usually available only in spring. You'll need 3 pounds of seed per 1,000 square feet—more if you are planting bunchgrasses and want a thick stand right away. If you use plugs, plan on one or two per square foot.

3 CLEAR THE EXISTING VEGETATION. Use one or a combination of the following methods: repeat tilling, sodcutting, smothering, or herbicide.

If you use tilling, cultivate two or three times, about a week apart. A sodcutter is a piece of power equipment that you can rent. It strips off the top layer of grass and roots, leaving a nearly weed-free planting area.

Alternatively, you can smother and kill the vegetation by covering it with black plastic, old rugs, or boards. The cover must be in place through an entire growing season.

The recommended herbicides are broad-spectrum, nonpersistent ones, such as glyphosate (Roundup or Ranger). Follow label instructions. It usually takes two to three weeks for all vegetation to die.

4 ASSESS THE SOIL FERTILITY. Unless the site is extremely infertile and compacted, no amendments are required. If the soil is heavy and clumps together, spread a two-inch layer of compost and till or mix it in.

5 RAKE THE AREA SMOOTH. Break up all clumps. Reserve some soil from the area in a pile or wheelbarrow to lightly spread over the seeds after they are sown.

Step 7: Mix seeds with sand or another inert material and hand broadcast.

Steps 8 and 9: Rake gently to cover the seeds and then roll the surface.

Step 11: Water with a fine spray.

6   IF YOU ARE USING PLUGS, PLANT THEM. If you are using a mixture of plugs and seed, plant plugs first. Space them on 12-inch centers and then scatter seed around them. If you are using only plugs, plant on 6- to 8-inch centers—two plants per square foot.

7   IF YOU ARE USING SEEDS, PLANT THEM. For small areas (less than 2,000 square feet), mix seed with sand or an inert material, such as peat moss or vermiculite, that has been slightly dampened. For a 1,000-square-foot area, use a bucket that's about the size of a bushel. Hand broadcast half of the bucket's contents over the site by walking in one direction. Then spread the second half, walking in a perpendicular direction. For large areas, use a drill seeder.

Spring seeding favors warm-season grasses and fall-flowering forbs; late-summer seeding favors cool-season grasses and spring-flowering forbs.

8   RAKE THE SURFACE. Rake gently to mix in the seed and cover it with soil, only ¼- to ½-inch deep. Broadcast the reserved soil mixture over any spots where the seed is exposed.

9   ROLL THE AREA. This ensures that seeds have firm contact with the soil.

10   MULCH WITH STRAW. Scatter a light layer of chopped, clean, weed-free straw (*not* hay).

11   WATER. Use a fine sprinkler head, to keep from dislodging the seed or causing runoff.

Step 14: Control weeds by hand pulling them when they first emerge.

⑫ **KEEP THE SEEDBED MOIST.** Until seedlings emerge, the seedbed should be moist but not soaked. You may need to water every day or every other day if it doesn't rain. Many factors affect the rate of germination but, in most cases, you should see seedlings in 10 to 15 days. Continue to irrigate through the first year. Once the grasses are established, irrigation will not be necessary.

⑬ **CHECK THE SITE EVERY DAY.** Your grass seedlings will have long, thin leaf blades. If you see any broadleaf weeds—plants with rounded leaves—pull them immediately.

⑭ **CONTROL WEEDS BY HAND PULLING WHEN THEY FIRST EMERGE.** If weeds are too close to a grass seedling to pull without disturbing it, clip the weeds at ground level. If weeds grow taller than the grass, cut the entire area (no lower than 4 inches) with a string trimmer. You may need to do this once a month during the first year. However, at the end of the season, just before winter, it is best not to cut off the growth, which helps protect the young plants from extreme weather.

PLANTING & MAINTAINING

A BUFFALOGRASS

LAWN

TERRANCE P. RIORDAN

BUFFALOGRASS (*Buchloë dactyloides*) has prospered on the Great Plains for centuries. This native grass is a sod-forming species and uses water efficiently, having adapted over thousands of years to the periodic and prolonged droughts characteristic of the region. Today, an increasing number of people are using this short, fine-leaved prairie grass as an ecologically sound and energy-efficient alternative to conventional turf. A warm-season grass, it spreads by both seed and stolons (runners), which take root and produce new plants.

Buffalograss is usually dioecious, meaning male and female flowers occur on separate plants. The inflorescences on male plants are one-sided spikelets on stems that rise 3 to 8 inches above the leaves. Female plants produce one or more burrlike inflorescences that remain partially hidden among the leaves near ground level; each burr contains one or more seeds.

Buffalograss starts growing in early May and begins to go dormant in early fall in the Central Plains. Leaves are blue-green during the growing season, although there is great variation not only in leaf color but also leaf width and internode length (the distance between leaves on the stem). Buffalograss does not tolerate excessive shade and is not well adapted to

BUFFALOGRASS

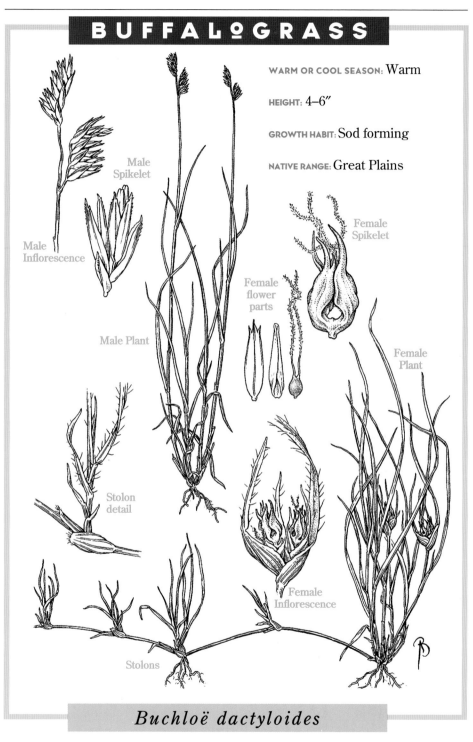

WARM OR COOL SEASON: Warm

HEIGHT: 4–6″

GROWTH HABIT: Sod forming

NATIVE RANGE: Great Plains

Male Spikelet

Male Inflorescence

Female Spikelet

Female flower parts

Male Plant

Female Plant

Stolon detail

Female Inflorescence

Stolons

Buchloë dactyloides

sandy soils. Once established, it can survive in saturated soils for short periods of time. Its extensive, deep root system and relatively low water use make it highly resistant to drought stress. Monthly irrigation in summer normally will prevent the plant from going dormant. Buffalograss, especially the new cultivars developed for use as a lawn, makes it possible for many Americans, particularly those in the prairie and plains states where it is native, to have high-quality turf that requires very little work and vastly less water and fertilizer than the widely cultivated, nonnative, cool-season turfgrasses. Buffalograss is particularly well suited to the transition zone of the United States. This is the zone where often it is too hot for cool-season turfgrasses and too cold for warm-season species.

ESTABLISHING A BUFFALOGRASS LAWN

There are three ways to start a buffalograss lawn: with seed, plugs, or sod. Seed of several improved turf-type cultivars is available in bulk. Be sure to specify primed seed, which has been soaked or treated with KNO_3, a relatively nontoxic salt, to help soften the seed coat and break dormancy. Plugs are helpful when immediate soil stabilization is important. Using sod, although expensive, will vastly decrease the time required to cover the planted area.

No matter which method you use, it is important to properly prepare the site to get the lawn off to a good start.

Preparing the Bed

If the soil has been compacted by vehicles or extensive foot traffic, rotary till to promote deep rooting. If you are planting seed, work the soil to a gardenlike but firm condition; in other words, the seedbed should be firm enough to walk on without sinking more than ½ inch into the soil. This can be accomplished mechanically with a light lawn roller or by irrigating the soil before seeding. If you use plugs or sod, a gardenlike condition is preferable but not as important, provided the plug or sod has good contact with the soil.

Eradicate all vegetation in the planting area by tilling or applying herbicide. Control early-season weeds by tilling before seeding. An application of a nonselective herbicide, such as Roundup, is recommended before establishing plugs. Follow all instructions and restrictions on the label when applying herbicides.

Fertilizing

Although adapted to a wide range of soil types, buffalograss is best suited for naturally fertile, clay and loam upland soils. It will establish and grow

Buffalograss, especially new cultivars such as this '609' in Dos, Texas, is a high-quality turf that needs little water, fertilizer, or mowing in its native range.

BUFFALOGRASS CULTIVARS
FOR THE UNITED STATES

'118': Excellent turf performance in the southern and transition zones of the U.S. Available only as sod of a female plant.

'315': Good turf performance in the northern and transition zones of the U.S. Available only as sod or plugs of a female plant.

'378': Excellent turf performance in the northern and transition zones of the U.S. Available only as sod or plugs of a female plant.

'609': Excellent turf performance in the southern and transition zones of the U.S. Available only as sod of a female plant.

'BISON': Good turf performance in the northern and transition zones of the U.S. Available only as a seed mixture of both male and female plants.

'CODY': Excellent turf performance in all zones of the U.S. Available only as a seed mixture of both male and female plants.

'LEGACY' (61): Excellent turf performance in the northern and transition zones of the U.S. Available only as sod or plugs of a female plant.

'PLAINS': Good turf performance in the southern and transition zones of the U.S. Available only as a seed mixture of both male and female plants.

'PRAIRIE': Good turf performance in the southern and transition zones of the U.S. Available only as sod of a female plant.

'SHARP'S IMPROVED': Good turf performance in the northern and transition zones of the U.S. Available only as a seed mixture of both male and female plants.

'STAMPEDE': Good turf performance in the southern and transition zones of the U.S. Available only as sod of a female plant.

'TATANKA': Excellent turf performance in the northern and transition zones of the U.S. Available only as a seed mixture of both male and female plants.

'TEXOKA': Good turf performance in the northern and transition zones of the U.S. Available only as a seed mixture of both male and female plants.

'TOPGUN': Excellent turf performance in the southern and transition zones of the U.S. Available only as a seed mixture of both male and female plants.

The **SOUTHERN ZONE** includes the southwest quarter of New Mexico, the southern half of Arizona, and the southeastern edge of California south of Death Valley. The southern zone also includes Florida, coastal Alabama and the area south of a line extending from Hattiesburg, Mississippi, west to Ft. Davis, Texas. The **TRANSITION ZONE**'s southern boundary is that same line, and its northern boundary extends across the country from Washington, D.C., west to Monterey, California. The **NORTHERN ZONE** includes all of the area north of that line.

Bulbs add color to a buffalograss lawn in spring when the grass is still dormant.

in areas with eroded soils, and often does well in infertile or poorly drained soils. Apply a starter fertilizer high in phosphorus when seeding to enhance seedling root development and stolon growth. Nitrogen is also important for early growth.

Seeding

For large areas, use a depth-limiting drill, which plants burrs at a depth of ½ inch or less. Use a 1- to 2-inch row spacing. For smaller areas, broadcast seed by hand. Assure proper soil-seed contact by using a harrow or by hand raking, first in one direction and then in a perpendicular direction. Rolling the area before watering is helpful.

Late spring is the optimum time to seed. If you seed at this time, you should have a full stand by September. Seeds will not germinate until soil temperatures reach 60°F. This is usually around May 15 in the central plains, but may differ in your particular climate. It is important to control early-season weeds before spring seeding (see "Preparing the Bed," page 18). Irrigation during germination and throughout the first growing season will greatly increase your chances for success.

For best results, don't sow buffalograss after August 15; unirrigated fall seedings of buffalograss when soil temperatures are greater than 50°F often fail because young seedlings are susceptible to frost damage and winter drying. Areas that cannot be irrigated can be seeded in the fall or winter, after soil temperatures fall below 50°F.

The amount of seed required depends on many factors. Trials conducted in Nebraska indicate that rates of 1 to 3 pounds of burrs per 1,000 square feet, seeded in early June, produce fully covered stands by mid-September. A good rule of thumb is 2 pounds of burrs per 1,000 square feet.

Planting Plugs

Plugs should be 2 inches or more in diameter with a minimum depth of 2½ inches. Spacing can vary, depending upon how quickly you want full coverage, but should be no farther than 24 inches on center. During the first year when the lawn is becoming established, it is important to keep weeds to a minimum. Periodic mowing at a height of 2 to 3 inches will help minimize weed competition.

Plugs are available either prerooted or not prerooted. Prerooted plugs have been harvested from an established field, placed in trays, fertilized, and watered in a greenhouse or under clear plastic for 4 to 8 weeks. For early spring and summer planting, they have been shown to establish more quickly than those that have not been prerooted. Plugs harvested in March, prerooted, and planted in May will, under proper growing conditions, establish an acceptable stand by fall.

Plugs that are not prerooted need 3 to 4 weeks to initiate growth and may not provide complete cover by fall. Newly harvested plugs may "go brown" after planting due to transplant shock. It is possible to minimize this off-color period and ensure good rooting by applying a starter fertilizer at 1 pound phosphorus and 1 pound nitrogen per 1,000 square feet at planting time and irrigating while the plugs are becoming established.

Planting Sod

Irrigation and fertilization requirements for sod are the same as for a plug planting. Sod, like newly harvested plugs, may exhibit an off-color appearance during the first few weeks after planting.

Selecting Plugs and Sod

When selecting plugs or sod you will have a choice of cultivar and either male or female plants. A single-cultivar lawn will be more uniform than one that includes several varieties. However, as when selecting any turfgrass, it is important to choose a cultivar that is resistant to pests and diseases.

Another important decision is whether to select a cultivar with one or both genders. In unmowed lawns, the male flowers, which generally extend above the leaf blades, are visible, and so some people consider them undesirable. By contrast, female flowers remain close to the ground and are not as visible. To have all-female plants, you must start your lawn

A comparison of two lawns in Texas: Water-guzzling, high-maintenance St. Augustinegrass (left) and drought-tolerant, native buffalograss '609' (right).

with plugs or sod, not seed. If you're planning on mowing, the choice of using either a female cultivar or a male/female cultivar is moot because the flowerheads will be trimmed off.

Irrigation

After seeding, water lightly (¼ to ½ inch), depending on present soil moisture and natural precipitation. Subsequently, water only to maintain a slightly moist surface and adequate subsoil moisture. This also helps reduce weed competition. With treated seed, seedlings emerge in 10 to 14 days. Water plugs and sod every other day for the first week, and every third day the second week. Water once a week the third through the fifth weeks, if there has been less than ¼ inch of rainfall since the previous irrigation. Do not let water puddle or run off. Establishment will take longer without watering.

On hot days, light watering (syringing) in the late morning or early afternoon will improve stolon growth and rooting in plants established from all methods. Syringing is a light application of water (⅛ inch or less) to prevent wilt and to cool the turf.

Weed Control

Your greatest challenge in establishing a buffalograss lawn will be weed control. Remove weeds from the bed before planting. Eliminate as quickly as possible any weeds that develop after the buffalograss has been seeded. Weeds taller than buffalograss seedlings should be mowed at a height of 2 to 3 inches. Hand weeding is effective for smaller areas.

Insects

In general, buffalograss is relatively free of insect and mite pests. This may be because established buffalograss usually harbors many beneficial insects—big-eyed bugs, syrphid flies, lady beetles, predatory mites, and several species of parasitic wasps—that naturally control pest populations.

The most potentially serious buffalograss pests identified so far are a tiny, grass-infesting mealybug, the buffalograss webworm, and a short-winged species of chinch bug. However, there are no insecticides registered to control these pests on buffalograss. Control them with proper maintenance and cultural practices.

Diseases

Buffalograss is relatively disease free. Isolated cases of diseases have been reported, but little research has been done in this area. Proper maintenance of buffalograss should reduce the likelihood of disease.

MAINTAINING A BUFFALOGRASS LAWN

Irrigation

After the first year, buffalograss lawns in Nebraska usually can be maintained with no irrigation beyond rain, though the quality of the lawn may be enhanced with some timely irrigation. During especially dry springs, irrigation when the turf begins to green up will insure a vigorous, dense lawn that can outcompete weeds.

Supplemental water is most beneficial in late July through August, the period of active stolon growth. Irrigation at this time helps stolons develop roots at the nodes, thus establishing new plants. Unfortunately, it also promotes weed growth. The lawn's green color can be somewhat extended in the fall with additional water, before freezing temperatures arrive.

Fertilizing

For best results, fertilize between June 15 and 30. Nitrogen levels should not exceed 1 to 3 pounds per 1,000 square feet per year, depending on the length of the growing season in your area. Buffalograss will provide a good quality turf with up to 1 pound per 1,000 square feet of nitrogen annually.

Because buffalograss—particularly cultivars like 'Prairie', shown here—is naturally short, no mowing is required. In fact, the more you mow, the more supplemental water will be necessary to maintain a thick, green turf.

Mowing

Because buffalograss is naturally short, no mowing is required. You can mow to a height of 3 to 4 inches to remove the slender male flower stalks that rise above the leaves. This may require regular mowing, since the male flowers are continually produced. Female selections require less mowing.

For a uniform appearance, mow at a height of $2\frac{1}{2}$ inches at 3- to 4-week intervals in late spring and 2- to 3-week intervals later in the season.

The more you mow, the more supplemental water will be required to maintain a thick, green turf. Minimal mowing and higher cutting heights promote a vigorous root system. Removal of more than one-third of the leaf will reduce root activity and growth, making plants more susceptible to moisture stress near the soil surface. Do not cut the grass by more than one-third its total height at any one mowing.

LOW & SLOW

FESCUES

STEVIE DANIELS

FOR YEARS THE FINE FESCUES languished as obscure players in the turfgrass pantheon, relegated to second-class status as components of shade-tolerant seed mixtures. These attractive, fine-textured grasses are finally coming into their own.

Today, fine fescues are being hailed for their low maintenance requirements. They grow slowly and if left uncut reach a mature height of only 8 to 12 inches. They don't like a lot of fertilizer, and thrive in dry, infertile soil. They tolerate not only partial shade but also drought. In fact, irrigation and fertilizer actually *restrict* their development. Fine fescues can withstand the cold of northerly climes and the heat of the upper South. They have fine, narrow leaves to boot.

The two main types of native fine fescues are red fescue (*Festuca rubra*) and sheep fescue (*F. ovina*). Many subspecies and cultivars of red fescue have been developed for use in turfgrass blends. A natural variety of sheep fescue commonly known as hard fescue, *F. ovina* var. *duriuscula,* is sometimes listed as *F. longifolia*. Hard fescue is described in some sources as native to open woods and stony slopes from North Dakota and Washington to Alaska; it apparently was introduced and naturalized east-

RED FESCUE

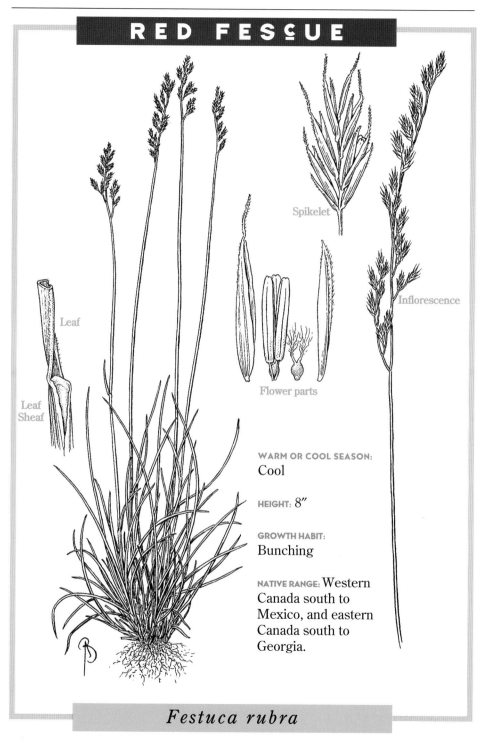

Spikelet

Leaf

Leaf
Sheaf

Inflorescence

Flower parts

WARM OR COOL SEASON:
Cool

HEIGHT: 8″

GROWTH HABIT:
Bunching

NATIVE RANGE: Western
Canada south to
Mexico, and eastern
Canada south to
Georgia.

Festuca rubra

ward. It is also native to Europe. Many states have other indigenous fescues, although these have not been cultivated by nurseries or horticulturists and seed is not commercially available.

Both red and sheep fescues are bunchgrasses, meaning that each plant forms a small clump. Consequently, if you plant the pure species, you will need to sow thickly to get a dense cover (6 pounds per 1,000 square feet). The subspecies and cultivars of red fescue that have been developed for use in turfgrass mixtures send out runners and therefore form a sod. These include creeping red fescue (*F. rubra* subsp. *trichophylla*), spreading fescue (*F.r.* subsp. *rubra*), and chewings fescue (*F.r.* subsp. *commutata*). They do not need to be seeded as thickly, so use 5 pounds per 1,000 square feet.

The popular, small ornamental grass blue fescue is a cultivar of sheep fescue. You may see it labeled *F. ovina* 'Glauca' or *F. cinerea*. In fact, dozens of blue fescue cultivars have been developed, ranging in height from 5 to 15 inches, and most send up silvery green seed heads in early summer. These inflorescences turn beige and shatter by midsummer.

GROWING FINE FESCUES

Fine fescues are cool-season grasses that do best in the middle Atlantic region and farther north or in high-altitude regions of the middle to lower South. They prefer slightly acid soil (5.5 to 6.5 pH). They green up early in the spring and stay green longer in the fall than warm-season grasses do; they're even evergreen in some situations. They germinate rapidly (in five to twelve days), and seedlings establish quickly.

Prepare the ground before sowing (see "Planting a Native Grass Lawn Step by Step," beginning on page 11). The best time to sow is August to September.

All blue fescue cultivars are propagated solely from division (not from seed) to maintain their characteristics. Therefore, if you want to use them as a groundcover you will need to start with plants. They look their best when trimmed in fall or early spring before new growth begins. Clip the foliage 3 to 4 inches above the crown but do not cut back hard, especially in the heat of summer. Sometimes old clumps die out in the center after three to four years. You can divide and replant the sections or plant new plants. Keep in mind that if you start with a cultivar propagated by division and let it go to seed, the new seedlings may not be exactly like the original plant. For instance, the foliage may not be as blue.

Left unmowed, the "no-mow" mix of hard and creeping red fescues forms a soft carpet of grass for cooler, medium-rainfall areas of the Midwest and Northeast.

NO-MOW MIX

One commercially available fine fescue seed mix was developed by Neil Diboll, chairman of Prairie Nursery in Westfield, Wisconsin. Diboll, known for his expertise in designing and establishing prairie plantings, realized that although many people may not want to fuss with a highly manicured lawn, they still want some kind of low-growing, green play area—one that does not require mowing or applications of fertilizers and herbicides. He experimented with various fescues and came up with a "no-mow" lawn mix suitable for the cooler, medium-rainfall areas of the upper Midwest and northeastern United States, and southern Canada. The mix contains hard fescue and creeping red fescue. He recommends sowing 5 pounds per 1,000 square feet. The no-mow mix will not do well in poorly drained soil, wet soil, or heavy clay.

Left unmowed, the no-mow lawn will form a soft, 4- to 6-inch-tall carpet of grass. If you prefer a more cropped look, mow once a month to a height of 3 to 4 inches. Never remove more than one-third of the top growth; cutting lower may damage the grasses. Water only during dry periods—occasional thorough soakings are better than frequent light sprinklings. Fertilizer is not necessary.

Red fescue, like all the fine fescues, thrives in spots where other turf-grasses would languish.

TURFGRASS CULTIVARS

Some special fine fescues were developed by Jan Weijer, a plant geneticist retired from the University of Alberta. He collected all sorts of native grasses growing on the cold and dry eastern slopes of the Canadian Rockies. The cultivars he developed, which are not yet named or available on the market, are frost and drought tolerant and grow only 6 to 7 inches a year. They are not naturally sod forming, so they must be seeded heavily to get a closely spaced lawn.

The easiest way to achieve a thick lawn is to let the grass go to seed the second year of growth, according to Weijer. "Let the grasses reseed themselves, filling in whatever gaps there may be," he advises. He says in the test plots that he established, only two annual mowings were necessary—one early in spring to remove debris, and one after flowering to remove spikelets.

Some good fine fescue varieties to seek out at your local garden center are 'Jamestown II' and 'Warwick', both types of chewings (red) fescue; and 'Falcon', 'Spartan', 'Reliant', 'Waldina', and 'Scaldis', all types of sheep fescue. They are all creeping or spreading grasses and should be sown at a rate of 5 pounds per 1,000 square feet.

SEDGE

LAWNS FOR
EVERY LANDSCAPE

JOHN GREENLEE

F EW BREAKTHROUGHS in the history of turf have been as significant as the arrival of an entirely new kind of lawn—the sedge lawn. Sedges are close botanical cousins of the grasses and look a lot like them. Properly selected and planted, sedges can function as a traditional lawn, yet they require little or no mowing, fertilizing, or chemicals. Some require less water than many conventional turfgrasses. Others tolerate wet, moist areas, and many thrive in shade. What's more, sedge lawns restore something of the character of the native sods that existed before agriculture and development transformed the American landscape.

Conventional lawns consist of grasses from Africa, Asia, Europe, and other places. These foreign, high-maintenance species have largely replaced the native sods composed of sedges and grasses. Today very little remains of the native sods. Perhaps the new American lawn is the original sod just waiting to be rediscovered.

Part of the attraction of the genus *Carex*, into which sedges fall, is its tremendous variety and adaptability. There are more than 2,000 species of *Carex*, and they are found in a wide range of habitats in nature. They vary from miniatures with foliage only 1 to 2 inches high, to specimens growing to 3 or 4 feet. Some creep, some clump, some do a little of both. They can be found in sun or shade, in wet soils or heavy clay, from coastal dunes to alpine scree. In almost every ecosystem, there is at least one sedge with good, lawnlike qualities.

Five sedges that have shown excellent promise as substitutes for traditional lawngrasses are catlin sedge (*Carex texensis*), Texas Hill Country sedge (*C. perdentata*), Baltimore sedge (*C. senta*), Pennsylvania sedge (*C. pensylvanica*), and California meadow sedge (*C. pansa*). These species are described below.

These native sedges have been selected for their compact growth and good, green color; most are evergreen as well. Many will tolerate varying degrees of shade and competition from tree roots. They are best grown in the regions where they are native, although most have shown amazing adaptability and grow well in regions outside their native range. As more horticulturists become aware of the sedges' potential in gardens, many more species are being collected from remnant populations in nature. Hybridization is still untapped and offers enormous possibilities for lawns of the future.

Carex texensis
CATLIN SEDGE

This wide-ranging sedge is found in nature from Texas through Ohio and has naturalized in parts of southern California. In nature, it hybridizes and mingles with closely related, similar species throughout the Southeast. Catlin sedge is adapted to a wide variety of climates, from the hot, muggy Southeast to the hot, dry Southwest. It is hardy to USDA Zone 6, and perhaps Zone 5 in sheltered locations. It forms a matlike clump 3 to 4 inches high and 6 inches wide. To maintain as a lawn, catlin sedge will require two to three mowings per year. This dark green sedge is at its best in partial to full shade. Planted in full sun, it will tend to be lighter green and require ample water to look its best. Catlin sedge makes a fine lawn mowed or unmowed, planted either from seed or from plugs 6 inches on center.

Carex perdentata
TEXAS HILL COUNTRY SEDGE

This Texas native is another excellent lawnlike sedge. It is drought tolerant and moisture tolerant with surprisingly soft, medium-green foliage.

PENNSYLVANIA SEDGE

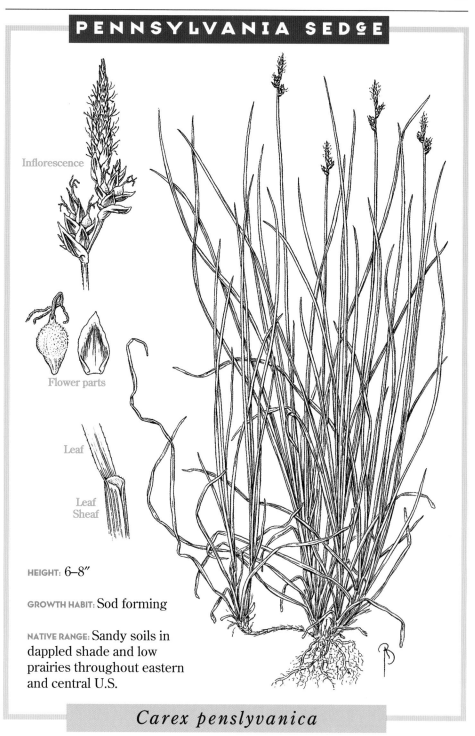

Inflorescence

Flower parts

Leaf

Leaf
Sheaf

HEIGHT: 6–8″

GROWTH HABIT: Sod forming

NATIVE RANGE: Sandy soils in dappled shade and low prairies throughout eastern and central U.S.

Carex penslyvanica

PLANTING SEDGE LAWNS

Sedge lawns are usually planted from plugs, as the seeds of many sedges are short lived and have low germination rates. The most important step in establishing a new sedge lawn is to start with weed-free soil.

When converting an existing lawn, make absolutely sure the old lawn is dead (see "Planting a Native Grass Lawn Step by Step," beginning on page 11). Top-dressing newly planted plugs is far more beneficial than incorporating mulch into the soil. Fertilize as you would a lawn to speed establishment. Mowings every month in the growing season will speed tillering and help the newly planted plugs to fill in.

Its slowly creeping, almost clump-forming foliage is a light green color growing 4 to 6 inches high. A very versatile sedge, *C. perdentata* grows equally well in sun or shade, heavy or sandy soils. Its evergreen foliage is dependably hardy to Zone 6 and possibly lower. It looks best when watered regularly, but like most sedges it will tolerate periods of summer drought. Plant from plugs 6 to 12 inches on center in fall or spring.

Carex pensylvanica
PENNSYLVANIA SEDGE
Pennsylvania sedge has a wide distribution throughout the eastern and central U.S., with one form, *C. pensylvanica* var. *pacificum*, reaching all the way to Puget Sound in Washington state. With such a wide distribution in nature, this sedge and its hybrids hold much promise for natural lawns of the future. Many distinct and varied clones are being evaluated by nurseries throughout the country. Typically found on sandy soils in dappled shade or as a constituent of low prairies, Pennsylvania sedge can tolerate less than ideal conditions in the garden. Its noninvasive, creeping foliage forms dense mats of medium green, fine-textured foliage growing 6 to 8 inches unmowed. As a mowed lawn, this sedge looks best cut two to three times per year at 3 to 4 inches high. Plant Pennsylvania sedge from plugs 6 to 12 inches on center in fall or spring.

Carex pansa
CALIFORNIA MEADOW SEDGE
This native Pacific Coast sedge is hands-down one of the finest native sedges for making natural lawns. Largely untested in the East, it has proven durable in Texas and Colorado. Slowly creeping, dark green

California meadow sedge is evergreen in all but the coldest climates, and grows 4 to 6 inches unmowed. This informal lawn planting with spring bulbs is in Pomona, California.

foliage grows 4 to 6 inches unmowed. California meadow sedge will tolerate varied types of soil conditions and temperatures, from sandy, exposed seacoasts to heavy clays and hot, inland valleys. It is also exceptionally traffic tolerant. Thriving in full sun to partial shade, it will thin out in deep shade. Mowing two to three times per year keeps the foliage low, tight, and lawnlike. Unmowed, it makes an attractive meadow and remains evergreen in all but the coldest climates. California meadow sedge is fast to establish from plugs planted 6 to 12 inches on center.

Carex senta
BALTIMORE SEDGE

This native eastern sedge is essentially a refined version of catlin sedge—identical except for shorter flower spikes, which lend a neater, more lawnlike appearance when unmowed. Discovered originally by Briar Hoffman growing in the lawn of a church in Towson, Maryland, Baltimore sedge is one of the best low-growing, lawn-forming sedges for deep shade. Treat this sedge as you would *C. texensis* (see page 32). Plant plugs 6 to 8 inches on center. Like all sedges, plugs of Baltimore sedge planted in spring or fall will establish quickly.

JUNEᵍRASS

FOR DRY SITES ACROSS THE COUNTRY

STEVIE DANIELS

IN THE RAREFIED WORLD of turfgrass research, junegrass (*Koeleria macrantha*) is hot stuff. A native bunchgrass found in prairie, open woods, and sandy soil from Ontario to British Columbia, south to Delaware, Missouri, Louisiana, and California, junegrass has medium green, ribbonlike leaves and grows in tufts about 18 inches high.

One reason turfgrass scientists have become intrigued by junegrass is the performance of 'Barkoel', a cultivar introduced by Barenbrug Company, a Dutch corporation with branches in the United States, China, and Australia. "'Barkoel' makes a dense, low-growing, medium green turf," says Reed Funk, a Rutgers University breeder who spent 20 years developing the advanced-generation fescues and has become known as the "guru of grass seed." Although not native to the United States, 'Barkoel' has been included in turf trials at Rutgers University, New Jersey, since 1980. Funk says Rutgers researchers collected seed of junegrass growing in Eastern Europe and Mongolia and established it in test plots, but its performance has not been as good as that of 'Barkoel'.

William A. Meyer, another Rutgers University breeder, also sees a rosy

JUNEGRASS

WARM OR COOL SEASON: Cool

HEIGHT: 16–20″

GROWTH HABIT: Bunching

NATIVE RANGE: Prairie, open woods, and sandy soil from Ontario to British Columbia, south to Delaware, Missouri, Louisiana, and California

Inflorescence

Spikelet

Leaf

Leaf Sheaf

Flower parts

Koeleria macrantha

future for junegrass as turf. "Junegrass is an extremely good, low-maintenance grass," he says. "It does not want to be fertilized."

Leah Brilman, a plant geneticist with Seed Research of Oregon, regularly gathers seed from grasses in old parks, graveyards, and pastures
where plants persist without human help. On one outing, she collected
material that she thought was bluegrass, and later discovered was junegrass. Always on the lookout for a new, low-maintenance turfgrass, she is
now busy developing junegrass cultivars appropriate for use in a lawn setting. She says it will be at least five years before any are ready for release.

However, if you're the adventurous type, you garden on dryish soils in
the plant's native range, and you're looking for a low-maintenance,
drought-tolerant alterative to conventional turf, why wait?

GROWING JUNEGRASS

Junegrass prefers sandy and/or thin, gravelly soil—soil that tends to be
dry and not very fertile. In other words, fertilizing is not only unnecessary but can be downright detrimental. The turfgrass experts agree that
when it is fertilized, junegrass becomes too dense, puts out too many
tillers, and becomes susceptible to dollar spot, rust, and other diseases.

If you have a suitable site, how do you go about growing a junegrass
lawn? The best time to plant is early spring, before the soil has warmed
up. Junegrass is a cool-season species, and so its seeds will not germinate
once the soil is warm. You can, however, try seeding in the fall.

As is the case with any native grass you decide to plant, you must prepare the seedbed properly before sowing. Remove the existing grass and
weeds completely. (See detailed bed preparation instructions in "Planting
a Native Grass Lawn Step by Step," page 11.) For large areas, Meyer recommends sowing 125 pounds per acre. That translates into about 4 to 5
ounces per 100 square feet for smaller plots. Meyer also recommends
using a starter fertilizer (such as 10-10-10) at planting time, but never fertilizing again.

Keep in mind that bunchgrasses grow in clumps, leaving small gaps
between plants—unlike creeping species, which develop naturally into an
unbroken stand. You can scatter more seed of bunchgrasses to cover
those bare areas, or use the opportunity to plant low-growing wildflowers. Some good associates for junegrass are violets (*Viola* species),
prairie buttercup (*Ranunculus rhomboideus*), pasque flower (*Anemone
pulsatilla*), blue-eyed grass (*Sisyrinchium campestre*), and prairie smoke
(*Geum triflorum*). If you add wildflowers to your junegrass lawn, mow
only once a year, no lower than 4 inches.

Junegrass 'Barkoel', seeded in a small experimental plot, has spread and grown more vigorously than the Kentucky bluegrass that surrounds it.

You can mow junegrass every three or four weeks to keep it low, but if you leave it unmowed you will get to enjoy the glossy, silvery green, spikelike seed heads that the plants send up in early summer. Cut no lower than 3 inches. Or, if you are ready for a more natural look, cut the grass only once a year in early spring, before the bird and mammal nesting season. If you have a very large yard, you might want to mow narrow footpaths and along the boundaries with neighbors' properties. In the Rutgers trials, the junegrass has been mowed regularly, so Meyer could not give advice about its performance as an unmowed, low-growing grass. The same is true of Brilman's research.

After seeding junegrass, water lightly to keep the soil slightly moist. When junegrass becomes established, it only needs to be watered once a month in the summer.

JUNEGRASS MIXTURES

Because junegrass is a cool-season type, it stays green longer than the warm-season natives, which begin their growth in late spring, stay green all summer, and begin to go dormant and turn beige in fall. Brilman has not tried combining junegrass with other species, but said she thought an interesting experiment would be to mix cool-season fine fescues with warm-season blue grama (*Bouteloua gracilis*) and buffalograss (*Buchloë dactyloides*) to extend the length of time that the turf looks green. Junegrass could substitute for fine fescues as the cool-season grass in such a mix.

In its natural habitat—mixed-grass prairie—junegrass associates with little bluestem (*Schizachyrium scoparium*), needlegrass (*Stipa spartea*), and western wheatgrass (*Agropyron smithii*), as well as some short and tall prairie grasses, including buffalograss and sideoats grama (*Bouteloua curtipendula*).

Junegrass grows in clumps, leaving small gaps between plants. Use the opportunity to plant low-growing wild-flowers such as prairie smoke (left) or pasque flower (below).

Based on this knowledge, and in an effort to come up with a way to extend the length of green color in my lawn, I planted in my front yard an experimental blend of buffalograss, blue grama, and june-grass with a few sheep fescue (*Festuca ovina* 'Glauca') clumps scattered throughout. In late summer, it became apparent that the june-grass had not germinated well. So, in small pots I sowed seed of june-grass that I had reserved. In late September, when the

weather was beginning to cool off at night, I set the plants out. They are thriving this spring, and I am eagerly awaiting the silvery seedheads, which should appear in late May.

Unlike many of the other native grasses in this book, junegrass is a bit of an unknown. If you decide to experiment with it, you will be charting new territory. So, take notes and share what you discover.

LITTLE BLUESTEM

BLENDS FOR THE EAST

JAMES C. GRIMES

HEN I WAS GROWING UP on the eastern tip of Long Island, New York, little bluestem was everywhere. It is a major component of our maritime grasslands, where it mixes beautifully with the colors and textures of common sedge, crinkled hairgrass, and Maryland stiff aster. Little bluestem is a warm-season grass that is native throughout most of the United States and Canada. I had always taken this versatile native grass for granted and so never considered its potential as a lawn.

Then, several years ago, a young botanist named Eric Lamont and I were asked to replant the roughs and nonplay areas of a local golf course. We needed a mix of short native grasses that required no pesticides or irrigation and only occasional mowing. Lamont suggested little bluestem (*Schizachyrium scoparium*), common or Pennsylvania sedge (*Carex pensylvanica*), and tufted hairgrass (*Deschampsia flexuosa*), which he explained would create a maritime community. It sounded great. I began to see maritime grasses everywhere. I noticed lawns on older properties in the area—lawns that no one had planted but had emerged after years of only occasional mowing. They were the same maritime grasses and forbs Lamont had recommended. Vastly different from the Merion blue-grass sod typically used for turf in our area, these native lawns had more character and did not need irrigation or fertilization. They were fine on their own.

My investigation of these grasses has involved years of trial-and-error experimentation with many other native grasses and forbs. I've tried different ways of creating grasslands, propagating plants, and maintaining stands. Here are my best recommendations for success.

PREPARING THE SEEDBED

Grasses can be established from seed, plugs, divisions, or sod. As seed is the most commonly available and least expensive alternative, it is often best for large lawns or situations where budget makes other methods impractical. However, little bluestem, like many warm-season grasses, is fairly slow to establish from seed, taking two or three seasons to mature. Plugs, divisions, and sod will establish more rapidly and also give you the opportunity to place masses of tall or short grasses where you want them.

Analyze the suitability of the site

For little bluestem, direct sun is not just an option, it's a requirement. Warm-season grasses will not tolerate any shade. However, most warm-season grasses are fairly tolerant of poor soil. In sandy or dry soil, little bluestem tends to clump; in deeper, heavier soil, it spreads. If the lawn is going to be mowed regularly, the plant's habit of clumping or spreading is less significant. But if the grasses are not mowed regularly or if the desired effect is to let the plants grow and flower, rich soils may be a problem.

Bluestem isn't for every situation. Warm-season grasses tend to bend or fall over when grown with too much moisture. An alternative for more moist soils is broomsedge (*Andropogon virginicus*), which looks very much like little bluestem, except it is slightly taller and has leaves along the flower stem. In shady areas, where little bluestem would languish, I use tufted hairgrass and common sedge or some types of fine fescue.

Prepare the soil and control weeds

Soils can be adjusted to some degree to accommodate the desired grasses. When working in old farm fields, I routinely strip off a portion of the thick, heavy farm soil and supplement it with sand and organic matter. During this process, I vary the thickness and texture of soil throughout the site. Doing so creates conditions for a diverse plant community and a more natural effect.

LITTLE BLUESTEM

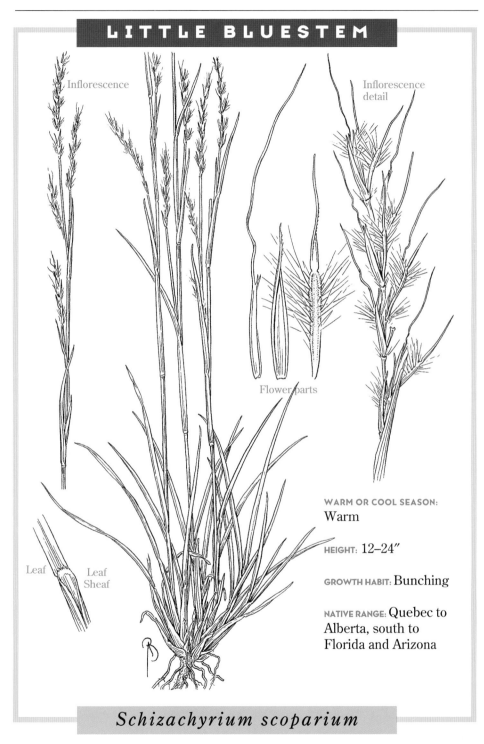

Inflorescence

Inflorescence detail

Flower parts

Leaf

Leaf Sheaf

WARM OR COOL SEASON: Warm

HEIGHT: 12–24″

GROWTH HABIT: Bunching

NATIVE RANGE: Quebec to Alberta, south to Florida and Arizona

Schizachyrium scoparium

Controlling weeds is the most important step in establishing a natural-looking grassland, especially when starting a native lawn in farm soil where undesirable growth has not been controlled. Omitting this step is a common but costly mistake. Weeds must be controlled for warm-season grasses to thrive, as they are not terribly aggressive in the seedling stage and are easily overrun by more aggressive broadleaf weeds and nonnative grasses.

Weeds can be controlled with mechanical or chemical means. Each approach has strengths and weaknesses.

I prefer to till if the soil needs to be amended or changed. On a small area, I remove the first 2 to 3 inches of soil, getting rid of most of the roots and seeds of undesirable plants. In farm soils, which in my area tend to be fairly fine-textured and poorly drained, I adjust the pH and amend with coarse sand and organic matter (approximately 1 to 2 inches of each). The areas are allowed to sit for several weeks to allow remaining weed seeds to germinate, and then the soil is tilled again. This process is repeated at least one more time to be sure all weeds are gone. The last tilling prior to seeding is very light—only 1 to 2 inches deep—to avoid bringing any remaining weed seeds to the surface.

One caution about repeated tilling: If the soil is fine-textured, tilling may destroy its structure, leaving you with soil that has the consistency of flour. Since you cannot repair the soil once it is pulverized, you may want to consider using a contact herbicide, such as Roundup, after the first tilling. Then, prior, to seeding, just scratch the surface with a rake.

If you are fortunate enough to have natural soil that has not been disturbed or areas that are already seeded as lawn, you may consider not tilling at all. In this situation, I use a contact herbicide spray to control unwanted growth. Woody shrubs are removed by hand.

If you prefer not to use chemicals and the area is small enough, you can cover it with black plastic to kill the existing growth. After the growth is dead, till the area lightly or rake prior to planting.

The length of time it takes to get rid of undesirable growth depends on a variety of factors. Optimally, having one full growing season to accomplish this task is worth the wait and is less costly in the long run.

SEEDING

Seeding of warm-season grasses differs from that of conventional cool-season lawn grasses. Cool-season grass seed tends to be small and clean, flowing easily through seeding equipment, such as broadcast seeders or standard lawn overseeders. But the physical character of warm-season

Little bluestem plugs started from seed collected from the wild help maintain some of the local gene pool. An area is planted with 2¼-inch plugs prior to seeding (right). The area after seeding is complete (below).

grass seed is different. A little bluestem, big bluestem, or Indian grass seed has a long, feathery appendage called an awn that gives the seed the texture of a goose feather. These seeds do not run smoothly through a gravity-fed spreader, and trying to hand broadcast the seed is like attempting to spread cottonballs. The seed literally bunches together, making it difficult to spread evenly or make good contact with the soil. However, there are several good alternative seeding methods for warm-season grasses.

Hydroseeding and drill seeding
Both hydroseeding and drill seeding work well for warm-season grasses. With hydroseeding, the seed is mixed in a large tank with water and a binder, such as paper pulp or newspaper fiber, and sprayed on the

ground. This method is most commonly used along roadsides, mall areas, and on steep slopes.

Drill seeding works well on large, flat, or rolling areas. A seed drill is a piece of equipment attached to a tractor. As it is towed along, it cuts a furrow, plants the seed approximately 1/4 to 1/2 inch deep, and closes the furrow. We use ours on expansive areas and existing grasslands where we want to add warm-season grasses or forbs.

There is one drawback to using a drill seeder: It places the seed on 6- to 8-inch centers, resulting in a "hair transplant" look. In spite of this, drill seeding is better than hydroseeding or hand seeding, as less seed is lost to the wind and birds.

Hand broadcasting

For small areas and touch-up seeding, we still hand broadcast. I usually mix the seed thoroughly with vermiculite or sand, especially when using a fine seed such as hairgrass or petticoat grass (*Eragrostis spectabilis*). This helps to spread the seed more evenly. After seeding, rough up the area to cover some of the seed. Then water well to provide good soil contact.

Seeding rates

Depending on the purity of the seed and whether you would like a pure stand or a mixture, the seeding rate will vary.

Warm-season and many native grasses tend to have quite a bit of chaff (anything that's not seed) mixed with the seed. This can have a dramatic effect on the actual amount of seed you are buying. Most recommended seeding rates are listed as PLS, for "pure live seed." For example, if you are trying to seed little bluestem, which is commonly about 40 to 50 percent PLS, at a rate of 25 pounds per acre, you will need between 50 and 60 pounds of bulk seed to plant 1 acre.

When ordering seed, specify your needs in PLS and most seed suppliers will provide it accordingly. If the supplier doesn't know what PLS is, usually you will get straight bulk seed. Just be sure the price reflects it. I've had a few occasions when the price was quoted as PLS but we received only the bulk amount.

WHEN TO PLANT

Sowing grasses at the proper time is based on an understanding of their life cycles. Warm-season and cool-season grasses have different growth patterns.

Left unmowed and mixed with wildflowers, little bluestem becomes a meadow.

Warm-season grasses break dormancy in late May. The plants' deep, well-developed root systems provide ample water through the hot growing season. As summer comes to an end, the plants go to seed. By the time the seeds are ripe, the cooler fall temperatures and shorter days prevent them from germinating. The seed overwinters in the soil and germinates when the soil warms up sufficiently the following summer.

Warm-season grasses need warm temperatures for both germination and growth. Spring seedings tend to favor the warm-season grasses and fall-flowering forbs (nongrass herbaceous plants).

Conventional lawn grasses, mostly cool-season types, emerge in spring and put on their growth during the cool, moist weather, usually flowering and setting seed by early summer. Most of these grasses go dormant during the hottest part of the summer. When late summer rains come, if any seed has developed and fallen to the ground, it will germinate in the warm weather of early fall and continue to grow in the cooler temperatures of late fall. Cool-season grasses germinate in warm temperatures and grow during cool temperatures.

Late summer and fall seedings favor the cool-season grasses and

NATIVE GRASSES AND GRASSLIKE PLANTS FOR THE NORTHEAST

Agrostis alba, Redtop
Carex pensylvanica, Pennsylvania or common sedge
Deschampsia flexuosa, Crinkled hairgrass
Eragrostis spectabilis, Petticoat grass or purple lovegrass
Festuca ovina, Sheep fescue
Festuca ovina var. *duriuscula*, Hard fescue
Festuca rubra, Red fescue
Juncus greenei, Greene's rush
Schizachyrium scoparium, Little bluestem

TALLER GRASSES FOR ACCENTS

Andropogon gerardii, Big bluestem
Panicum virgatum, Switchgrass
Sorghastrum nutans, Indiangrass

spring-flowering forbs. Temperatures are warm enough for both types of grasses to germinate, but the nights are cooler, a condition that makes the cool-season grasses thrive. Cool-season grasses, if not well established by the time hot weather arrives, will succumb to the heat.

I prefer to plant mixes that contain both warm-season and cool-season grasses with forbs in mid-August. The days are getting short enough and the nights are cool enough to prevent many of the annual weeds from germinating. But the temperatures are still warm enough for little bluestem and other warm-season grasses to germinate and develop before winter. Cool-season grasses germinate and grow well in these conditions. You can determine the success of the warm-season grasses by October, since, even though they are seedlings, they will still display their typical red fall color. If the germination rate seems light, scratch or drill in additional seed the following spring when the soil warms up.

Remember: Spring seeding favors warm-season grasses and fall-flowering forbs; late-summer seeding favors cool-season grasses and spring-flowering forbs.

The summertime green of little bluestem (left) becomes red as fall arrives (right).

Planting divisions, sod, and plugs

Divisions are produced by lifting established plants and dividing them into small sections. Care must be taken to maintain active growing points in each division. Divisions are commonly used to reproduce hybrids or a clonal selection that would not come true from seed. You can buy divisions of little bluestem and other grasses, but they tend to look stiff and unnatural. They only work well in spring when the plants are still dormant. Late-summer and fall divisions are prone to winterkill and not worth the effort.

Sod is an entire section of existing prairie that has been removed—everything that is growing, with as much root system as can be carried. You must have permission to do this kind of harvesting.

Plugging is the method I use most often. Plugs are small potted plants, usually propagated from seed. I take seed I have collected locally and pot up plugs to supplement seeded areas. The plugs can be planted before or after seeding and help us maintain some of the local gene pool in all our plantings. Little bluestem started in a greenhouse in winter will be large enough to bloom in August. Plugs are also available from several suppliers in a variety of sizes, from 1-inch cell packs, to peat pots, and larger containers.

For small areas, plugs can be more effective than seeding. Plugs can be planted any time during the growing season. Even though they are small, the 2-inch plants don't seem to be at a disadvantage and grow well even in the middle of summer, provided they have enough water when planted. Plugs also allow exact placement of plants. I use the chuck-and-duck method—throw the plugs out in a random fashion and plant them where they land.

MANAGING A NATIVE LAWN

The amount of maintenance a native grassland requires depends on the level of refinement to which you are accustomed or that you desire.

During establishment, expect some bare spots and weeds. Not all areas of a planting will establish at the same rate The same inconsistencies in soil and light that affect a traditional lawn will also affect a native grassland. I prefer to look at these trouble spots as opportunities for more diversity. These areas can be touched up with low-growing forbs that add seasonal color and texture to the grasses. A lovely companion for little bluestem is pussytoes (*Antennaria plantaginifolia*), which has woolly, whitish green leaves, grows only 1 to 2 inches tall, and is drought tolerant.

Although a native grassland only needs minimal care once it is established, it is not completely self-sustaining. If left unattended, over time it will evolve to more woody vegetation. To maintain the area as a grassland, some intervention will be necessary. Historically, grasslands in my area were burned every few years in the spring. The fire controlled woody weeds, such as bittersweet and honeysuckle, and helped control ticks. However, New York and other states have outlawed burning without a special permit, so mowing is a more common management tool.

Mowing requirements depend on your taste. Warm-season grasses like little bluestem can be mowed as low as 3 inches, but 5 inches is better. To create a more natural look and further minimize maintenance, I mow every week or so beginning in late April through the Fourth of July. This is the time when cool-season grasses put on most of their growth; if left too long between mowings, they may look shabby.

In June, hairgrass, by far the most graceful of any grass, sends up its wiry seed stalk. By early July, I stop mowing to allow the warm-season grasses and late-flowering forbs to develop. In high-traffic, high-visibility

A lawn of little bluestem and hard fescue that has been cut regularly and irrigated forms a beautiful green carpet of grass in August.

areas, I mow only as needed for a look that's informal but not seedy. The little bluestem and forbs, such as gayfeather (*Liatris spicata*) and asters (*Aster* species), will begin to flower and set seed, providing food for wildlife and self-sowing to fill in the grassland. Everything is left tall for the winter. The following April, I mow again and repeat the process.

Insects are an occasional problem in these grasslands but are usually not serious enough to warrant any action. Warm-season grasses have well-developed root systems, which help them endure insect attacks. Hard fescue and sheep fescue are more susceptible to injury. In areas where grubs are a consistent problem for cool-season grasses, we over-seed with warm-season grasses. During wet summers on irrigated sites, rust can sometimes be a problem. This is almost always related to how the site is being managed; cutting back on the amount of overhead water usually solves the problem.

Judicious neglect seems to be the best approach to native grasslands. All that's needed is occasional mowing. Since fertilizer seems to be the catalyst for most problems we've encountered, we only use a starter fertilizer during initial establishment and then feed only every other year or so if the grassland appears to be weak. If fertilization is necessary, we feed at only half the recommended rate.

WILDFLOWERS TO ADD AS ACCENTS

A native lawn of little bluestem is informal, durable, and beautiful, especially when accented with wildflowers. In spring, bits of color appear with the blooms of plants such as pussytoes (*Antennaria plantaginifolia*), blue-eyed grass (*Sisyrinchium angustifolium*), and bird's foot violet (*Viola pedata*). In July and August, when other lawns seem to shut down, little bluestem shows off its purple-blue seed stalks, then turns the color of red wine. This, combined with blooms such as those of white hyssop-leaved thoroughwort (*Eupatorium hyssopifolium*), Maryland aster (*Chrysopsis mariana*), yellow Maryland aster (*C. falcata*), purple gayfeather (*Liatris spicata*), blue stiff aster (*Aster linariifolius*), and heath aster (*A. ericoides*) creates an intriguing blend of fall color.

If taller spring wildflowers are used, mow the lawn early, before the flowers appear. Do not mow again until after the wildflowers bloom, and then use the mower to deadhead the flowers. —J.C.G.

Bird's foot violet (left)
and Maryland aster (below)

MEADOW GARDENS FOR THE NORTHEAST

WILLIAM A. NIERING

B Y CREATING A MINI-MEADOW on your homeground, you can help restore a habitat that was originally part of the Northeast landscape. I took this step on my own property, an acre in size.

The story begins in the early 1970s, some eight years after we moved to this hilltop in the small community of Gale's Ferry in the town of Ledyard, Connecticut. The site was an open field. The developer had created lawn around the house—the usual pattern. I was mowing one weekend with one of the noisiest power mowers available and undoubtedly disturbing my neighbor's party across the street. I imagined how I could develop a more environmentally friendly landscape that contained only a small lawn and needed minimum care.

First, to create greater privacy and decrease the lawn area, I planted tree and shrub borders along the property line. I used a mixture of evergreen and deciduous trees and shrubs, both native and introduced. I also included a screen of evergreen trees along the road in front of the house. Undulating border plantings such as these define and enclose a landscape, while reducing the mowed area at the same time. Although I try to avoid single-species plantings, my one exception is a border of arborvitae (*Thuja occidentalis*), which makes an excellent narrow screen where space is limited.

Planting tree and shrub borders need not be an expensive project. Plants can often be salvaged from vacant lots where development is planned or from friends who have extra trees and shrubs. For example, I salvaged red cedar, hemlock, flowering dogwood, and highbush blueberry.

Next, you may want to add to or change some of your foundation plants. You can include favorite shrubs, annual and perennial flowerbeds, and groundcovers. I eliminated considerable lawn with evergreen groundcovers that are also attractive in winter, such as pachysandra (*Pachysandra terminalis*). You could also use native groundcovers such as Allegheny spurge (*Pachysandra procumbens*) and wildflowers such as foamflower (*Tiarella cordifolia*). Consider the possibility of a vegetable garden, which should be planted in the sunniest spot.

A meadow can take up as much of the remaining area as you want; some people prefer no lawn, which is ideal. To create a meadow, you should favor the native grasses such as little bluestem, which thrives throughout the Northeast in dry, nutrient-poor soil. I favored it by using no fertilizer and no mowing, and I was lucky. Immediately after I stopped mowing, clumps of little bluestem became conspicuous. If you begin with a bare site, you could sow seed or plant small clumps to get your meadow started (see "Little Bluestem Blends for the East," page 41). We especially enjoy little bluestem during the fall and winter, when the clumps turn reddish tan, with showy flowerheads of fine, silver bristles. It is particularly striking after a light snow.

Over several decades, the meadow has been a constantly changing landscape. I have watched new plants appear and added ones I especially like. If a tree or unwanted shrub appears, such as black cherry, oak, or ash, I immediately pull it or dig it out by the roots. As the grasses and other plants become more dense, fewer woody plants appear. I have created a relatively stable, self-perpetuating meadow.

RESTORING AN ABANDONED FARM

In the early 1950s, the Connecticut College Arboretum in New London restored a naturalistic landscape on an abandoned farm. The goal was to accentuate and preserve some of the old field grasses and attractive native woody species that had naturally established after the farm was deserted. Today, after more than four decades, this beautiful meadow

A grassland of little bluestem forms the entrance to the naturalistic landscape area at Connecticut College Arboretum. Highbush blueberries, gray birch, and red cedar were favored by removing the less attractive species.

persists in a setting that would otherwise now be dominated by forest.

A grassland of little bluestem forms the matrix and entrance. This area was created by the selective removal of the less attractive woody species, such as black cherry (*Prunus serotina*), and the favoring of more attractive ones. Red cedar, highbush blueberries, huckleberry, gray birch, and flowering dogwood are among the species originally growing on the site. Although most would have been shaded out by the natural vegetation, these beautiful native shrubs and trees have been allowed to mature. Maintenance of the meadow has been minimal. A trail is kept open through the area so that plants can be observed at close range.

The meadow in an invaluable model for students and visitors to see firsthand how forest development can be arrested to maintain an open landscape that was originally part of the southern New England landscape. It also provides breeding habitat for a group of old field nesting birds, such as the Meadowlark, Bobolink, and Grasshopper Sparrow—species whose numbers have declined due to loss of habitat in North America. This biodiversity has given students opportunities to get involved in other, similar projects after they graduate. For instance,

Lucinda Young, working in Nantucket, Massachusetts, where she grew up, has written *Naturalistic Landscaping for Nantucket: An Ecological Approach*, in which she promotes this kind of landscaping for multimillion-dollar homes on the island.

Reversing the lawn mania in this country is the mission of a new organization that originated at Connecticut College—Smaller American Lawns Today (SALT), which encourages homeowners to transform at least some of their lawns into meadows or native woody plantings. Such efforts are part of a movement that aims to restore home backyards and industrial grounds to more ecologically sound and productive naturalistic landscapes.

MEADOW MANAGEMENT

Historically, grasslands were scattered throughout the oak-dominated forest of New England and the pine-oak forests of Long Island, New York. Burned periodically by pre-Colonial fires, the most extensive grassland was the Hempstead Plains on Long Island, comprising some 50 square miles. Only a remnant persists, under the ownership of the Nature Conservancy.

At the Connecticut College Arboretum, where I am the research director, we have used prescribed burning since 1968 to maintain little bluestem grassland and associated showy flowering plants (forbs), such as sweet goldenrod and wild indigo that increase with fire. Burning old fields to perpetuate little bluestem is increasing in Connecticut. In spring 1998, the forestry unit of the Connecticut Department of Environmental Protection burned 15 acres of grassland in Harkness Memorial State Park in Waterford, a large part of which was dominated by little bluestem. Obviously, however, the use of fire is restricted in many areas.

Mowing once or twice a year is an alternative that will also preserve grasslands. At Harkness Park, a twice-yearly mowing maintained the little bluestem grassland for nearly three decades. If summer mowing is needed, it should be done after July 15, the end of bird breeding season. If only one mowing is needed to suppress woody growth, early spring is recommended.

WHY NATURAL LANDSCAPES?

There are several reasons the movement toward natural landscaping is important ecologically. With minimum lawn, you can abandon the power mower for a reel mower, conserving fossil fuel and reducing noise and air pollution. Commercial fertilizers and pesticides can also be abandoned,

At Tower Hill Botanic Garden in Boylston, Massachusetts, a mowed walkway meanders through an unmowed meadow preserved for wildlife.

and—perhaps best of all—you will have more time to do other things.

In addition, you are undertaking a kind of ecological landscape restoration that favors old meadows, among the most endangered habitats in the Northeast. You are also contributing to biodiversity by creating habitat for life forms that are endangered by human activities. Decreasing the size of your lawn by adding trees, shrubs, and meadows invites wildlife, adding to the pleasure you find in your yard. You will see more birds, including hummingbirds, Rose-breasted Grosbeak, towhees, and Wood Thrush, as well as butterflies and other beautiful insects.

In an industrial world where natural landscapes are constantly disappearing, you have an opportunity to reverse the trend toward homogeneity and monocultures. Rather than relying on the fossil fuels and pesticides required for sustaining a manicured lawn, you can create a homeground that blends into the wilderness as a self-perpetuating system fueled by the sun. In this way, your naturalistic landscape will also help counter climatic warming. By restoring a natural landscape, you become part of a worldwide movement to minimize our impact on the acreage we actually need for our brief existence on this planet.

WILDFLOWERS TO ADD AS ACCENTS

Today, more than 25 years after I first replanted my Connecticut lawn with a meadow, it is more beautiful than ever. By mid-July, the meadow is ablaze with color and filled with insects, especially bees. I have added clumps of native bergamot, a beautiful lavender mint (*Monarda fistulosa*), purple blazingstars (*Liatris* species), black-eyed Susan (*Rudbeckia triloba*), sweet goldenrod (*Solidago odora*), wild indigo (*Baptisia tinctoria*), and ox-eye daisy (*Leucanthemum vulgare*). The last one is not native but has naturalized in this part of the country; I have promoted not only native species but also those that are frequently associated with postagricultural old field landscapes of southern New England.   **—W.A.N.**

Purple blazingstar (above) and goldenrod (left)

NATIVE GRASSES FOR THE
SOUTHEAST

WILL CORLEY

PLANT SUCCESSION MOVES at a rapid pace in the hot, humid Southeast. It only takes two or three years for dominant, aggressive species to overtake a plant community that has been disturbed or cultivated. It is no wonder, then, that the turf industry grows sod and seed of only five exotic grasses—they are the toughest barriers against the return of the original, vegetative state of mixed hardwood forests. However, these exotic turfgrasses also require exorbitant amounts of care and feeding.

As we begin to explore alternatives to high-maintenance turf for the region, two natural models surface: shortgrass and tallgrass prairies. In these settings, common bluestem (*Andropogon virginicus*) is ubiquitous. Paradoxically, although it is our most common grass, commercial seed (that is, seed sold in large quantities) for common bluestem is not widely available. An excellent substitute is common bluestem's slightly diminutive cousin, little bluestem (*Schizachyrium scoparium*). It grows to 2 feet in height, with bluish leaves and stems during spring and summer, turning bronzy orange during fall and winter. Silver bluestem (*Andropogon ternarius*) is similar in height and habit but less colorful.

NATIVE GRASSES FOR THE SOUTHEAST

Agrostis hyemalis
TICKLEGRASS
Understory grass to 2 feet with iridescent pink spring flowers. Sow at ½ ounce per 100 square feet.

Andropogon gerardii
BIG BLUESTEM
Sparse, tall grass to 7 feet with good fall foliage color. Sow seed at 4 ounces per 100 square feet, or 5 to 10 pounds per acre.

Andropogon ternarius
SILVER BLUESTEM
Thin clumps to 2 feet with bright silver blooms in fall and winter. Sow at same rate as big bluestem.

Andropogon virginicus
COMMON BLUESTEM
Robust, 3-foot clumps with good fall and winter color. Sow at same rate as big bluestem.

Eragrostis spectabilis
PURPLE LOVEGRASS
Understory grass to 2 feet with pink spring blooms. Sow at ½ ounce per 100 square feet, or one pound per acre.

Muhlenbergia capillaris
MUHLY GRASS
Stiff clumps to 3 feet with shocking pink late-fall color. Direct seeding of muhly grass is always disappointing, so it is usually plugged.

Panicum virgatum
SWITCHGRASS
Thin clumps to 4 feet with wispy panicles and light blue or green summer foliage. Sow at 3 ounces per 100 square feet, or 5 pounds per acre.

Schizachyrium scoparium
LITTLE BLUESTEM
Solid clumps to 2 feet, with light blue summer foliage that bronzes in late fall. Sow at same rate as big bluestem.

Sorghastrum nutans
INDIANGRASS
Coarse clumps to 5 feet with prominent straw color in winter. Sow at 4 ounces per 100 square feet, or 8 pounds per acre.

Tridens flavus
PURPLETOP
Thin, open clumps to 3 feet with purple-brown panicles in late summer. Good filler plant for taller grasses. Sow at 2 ounces per 100 square feet, or 4 pounds per acre.

Color peaks in fall in this meadow of bluestem grasses, goldenrod, and aster.

Establishment takes several years for bluestems, and so it is a good idea to add several faster-establishing species to a grass blend. Two of these bloom in midspring with iridescent pink inflorescences—purple lovegrass (*Eragrostis spectabilis*) and ticklegrass (*Agrostis hyemalis*). For erodible sites and those where a lower-growing lawn is desired, sideoats grama (*Bouteloua curtipendula*) or blue grama (*B. gracilis*) are excellent choices. This mix grows to approximately 2 feet and is colorful in spring, late summer, and fall. If mown, it should be cut no lower than 3 inches. Muhly grass (*Muhlenbergia capillaris*) is the most popular of the lower-growing ornamental grasses. Its pink color in fall is spectacular, even more dramatic than the spring bloom of purple lovegrass or ticklegrass. However, the higher cost of muhly grass will limit its use in landscapes.

A shortgrass prairie will inevitably be invaded by taller, more aggressive grasses and forbs. In some situations, you may want to add tallgrass prairie species to your mix—big bluestem (*Andropogon gerardii*), common bluestem, switchgrass (*Panicum virgatum*), Indiangrass (*Sorghastrum nutans*), and purpletop (*Tridens flavus*). The latter three mature during the initial growing season and fill in the lawn until the bluestems mature in two to three years.

A native shortgrass meadow is most colorful in spring to early summer. In tallgrass meadows, color peaks in late summer and fall. Native meadows provide habitat for songbirds, rabbits, and other small mammals. One pervasive fear is that the meadow will also be prime habitat for snakes; however, this fear is rarely substantiated.

PLANTING NATIVE GRASSES

After species selection, preparation of the planting site is of primary importance. Site preparation can be accomplished by multiple tillings through the summer, or overspraying the site with a contact herbicide in September and shallow tilling when sprayed vegetation has browned. After several rains, weed seedlings will probably appear. Apply the herbicide again, but do not till. Sow seedbeds in late fall and mulch with a weed-free material. You can also seed in spring if irrigation is a possibility. An initial application of general purpose fertilizer is helpful on very infertile planting sites. (For more on planting a native lawn, see page 11.)

Managing of native grasses and meadows is largely a matter of controlling invasive weeds and other undesirable plants. High mowings at 6 to 8 inches from spring through July are the most useful tool in weed control. Keep a sharp eye out for invasive grassy weeds such as crabgrass, goosegrass, and bermudagrass early in the spring. In March and April, you will have a narrow window of opportunity to overspray a grass-specific herbicide when the undesirable seedlings are most vulnerable to the herbicide and the native grasses are dormant. Occasional tall weeds can be hand pulled or spot sprayed during the growing season.

Cleanup mowing at winter's end is advisable. Mow no lower than 4 to 6 inches. On small sites, use a string trimmer or swing blade. When practical, burning can replace a mowing every few years. If fertilizer seems to be required, a light application in early summer is most beneficial.

As landscapes become less formal and environmental concerns grow more profound, native grasses are gaining popularity in the Southeast. Futurists envision managed prairies growing in landscapes where, a few centuries ago, Native Americans maintained their own grasslands and savannas for hunting.

WILDFLOWERS TO ADD AS ACCENTS

N ative wildflowers can be combined with grasses for a true meadow effect. Good choices for shortgrass meadows are Indian blanket (*Gaillardia aristata*), purple coneflower (*Echinacea purpurea*), lemon mint (*Monarda citriodora*), coreopsis (*Coreopsis* species), black-eyed Susan (*Rudbeckia hirta*), and showy primrose (*Oenothera speciosa*). In tallgrass communities, more aggressive species, including asters (*Aster* species), goldenrods (*Solidago* species), and sunflowers (*Helianthus* species), are appropriate. Whenever possible, select native wildflowers that are suited to the amount of moisture at the site, that complement the height of the native grasses, and that will not outcompete or be outcompeted by the grasses in the plant community.

—W.C.

Black-eyed Susan (above) and showy primrose (left)

NATIVE LAWNS FOR

FLORIDA

CRAIG HUEGEL

LTHOUGH MUCH OF FLORIDA was once a vast savanna with an understory dominated by grasses, it is rare today to find these grasses in cultivation. Native grass lawns or prairies have found little acceptance in modern Florida. While other areas of the country have waged successful battles against lawn ordinances that restrict native grasses and prairies, in most Florida suburbs, lawns may be grown no higher than 18 inches.

Although Florida receives more than its share of rainfall, the conservation of water is still a serious issue. In recent years, efforts to reduce water consumption have sparked interest in the use of native plants in gardens. Florida's native grasses have been an underused component of such landscapes, but their potential remains great. The species selected below are the best native grasses for Florida native lawns.

Aristida stricta
WIREGRASS
Prior to the development of urban and agricultural areas, wiregrass covered more than half of Florida. Nearly universal in areas that receive ade-

A wiregrass and wildflower meadow beneath longleaf pines in Apalachicola National Forest looks the way much of Florida appeared 400 years ago.

quate sunlight, it is the dominant understory grass in many of Florida's native plant communities. Wiregrass thrives in both the droughty soils of upland pine forests and the poorly drained soils of prairies. Because of its adaptability, wiregrass can be used in a wide variety of settings, except in coastal areas that receive direct salt spray or in areas where the soil pH is very high.

Wiregrass is a clumping, cool-season grass that begins growth in mid-January. Its thin, wiry leaves grow rapidly during the winter and spring but rarely grow taller than 15 inches in height. The seed heads form in May or June, reaching a height of 1 to 3 feet, and then growth ceases.

Wiregrass can be established either by seed or plants. Although seed was once largely unavailable, now it can be obtained from a number of sources. For best results, sow seed no deeper than 1 inch in bare soil and mulch lightly with grass clippings. With adequate watering, wiregrass germinates in about three weeks. The seedlings are relatively slow to establish. You can achieve results more quickly by using container-grown plants or by transplanting pieces of mature clumps. If plants are used, space them at least 2 feet apart.

Wiregrass is easy to maintain once established. It is exceptionally tolerant of both drought and periods of inundation, and it thrives in Florida's extremes of temperature and sunlight. If you want a mowed look, mow in early summer to remove the seed heads, but no lower than 12 inches.

Aristida spiciformis
BOTTLEBRUSH THREE-AWN
Bottlebrush three-awn is in the same genus as wiregrass, but it differs in several key respects. A warm-season grass, it produces most of its growth in late spring and summer. Its multiple, bristly, brushlike seed heads reach their mature height of 10 to 30 inches sometime between August and September. If allowed to mature, the awns catch in clothing. For this reason and to keep it looking tidy, this grass should be mowed no lower than 8 inches in midsummer.

Except for these differences, bottlebrush three-awn is similar to wiregrass. It is a bunching grass that stays green throughout the year and remains short when not in seed. In the wild, this grass is found throughout Florida in a wide variety of open habitats, ranging from sandy, well-drained sites to poorly drained sloughs. The recommendations for establishment and management of bottlebrush three-awn are similar to those for wiregrass. However, there are only a few commercial sources for seed or seedlings of bottlebrush three-awn.

Dichanthelium species
LOW PANICUMS, SWITCHGRASSES
The low panicums or switchgrasses were once considered a subfamily of the large genus *Panicum*, but today they are generally regarded as a distinct genus, *Dichanthelium*, due to their unique characteristics. Sixteen species are found throughout Florida, and any of them could be used as a lawn grass given the right conditions. These plants are all short in stature, rarely exceeding 18 inches in height, including their seed heads. They also all share a unique annual growth pattern with three distinct seasonal forms: the winter rosette, a spring growth form with ascending foliage and seed heads, and a summer or fall form that is prostrate with seed heads. During all phases, the foliage stays green.

Low panicums occur in a wide variety of habitats throughout Florida, but they are most common in the partial shade of an understory. They also thrive in areas where the soil has been disturbed. Low panicums are bunchgrasses, but their growth habit is spreading. Individual clumps can grow to a width of several feet. Over time, adjacent clumps tend to merge and become difficult to distinguish from each other.

As a lawn grass, low panicums grow best under filtered light. They are tolerant of varying degrees of moisture and are also durable, tolerating foot traffic. Maintenance of these species is also simple. Low panicums do not have to be mowed at all to keep them at 18 inches. However, one mowing in late spring will help keep the height uniform while the grass is growing vigorously.

Establishing low panicums is easy with either seed or plants, but neither is widely available. If you can find seedlings, I recommend using them; plant seedlings several feet apart the during the summer rainy season.

Eragrostis species
LOVEGRASSES

Within this rather large genus of grasses are several perennials whose size and habit make them appropriate for use in a lawn. All of these, however, are a bit coarser in the wild than the grasses listed above. Leaf blades of lovegrasses are flat (not needlelike) and a bit stiff to the touch. The plants themselves are more rigid. Nevertheless, lovegrasses are extremely adaptable and durable.

Coastal lovegrass (*Eragrostis refracta*) and Elliot's lovegrass (*E. campestre*) are similar, except that the latter has leaves that are somewhat silvery in color. Both species are 18 to 24 inches at mature leafheight, and the blooming season is between midsummer and early winter. Purple lovegrass (*E. spectabilis*) has beautiful purple seed heads, is several inches shorter, and flowers between August and November.

Although lovegrasses are perennial, they decline after flowering and do not maintain a lush appearance during winter. They also differ from the grasses described above by forming rhizomes from the base of each clump that allow the grass to expand outwards. Thus lovegrasses are rather quick to fill in an open spot in the lawn. This can be an advantage or a drawback, depending on your point of view.

A lawn of lovegrass will require some maintenance to keep it within the 18-inch standard, but this is easy to do as these grasses are tough and resilient to mistakes in mowing height. Establishment is simple from either seed or plants; if plants are used, space them at least 30 inches apart. Commercial availability of lovegrasses is limited, but a few nurseries are now offering both Elliot's and purple lovegrasses as seedlings and as container plants.

Oplismenus setarius
BASKETGRASS, WOODSGRASS
This grass differs greatly from all of those discussed here in its growth form and habits. A creeping grass, it spreads in all directions by forming roots periodically along the stem where it touches the soil surface. Basketgrass will quickly carpet an area that has little existing vegetation.

Basketgrass is found throughout Florida in moist, shady environments. Its use as a lawn grass, therefore, is restricted to such areas. It will thrive in shady spots where little else will grow, but will not expand to areas of the yard that receive full sun or where the soil is dry.

Basketgrass is a perennial that maintains its appearance throughout the year. Leaf blades generally are shorter than 3 inches and less than $\frac{1}{2}$ inch wide. Flowering can occur during any month. Basketgrass never grows higher than several inches, even in flower, so mowing is unnecessary. If conditions are favorable, however, it may become difficult to confine. In most cases, this is not a problem, as it is not overly aggressive and will not smother taller groundcovers.

Basketgrass is best established with small, container-grown plants spaced 2 to 3 feet apart during months with adequate rainfall. At this time, this grass is not widely available from commercial sources.

Sporobolus junceus
PINEWOODS DROPSEED
Pinewoods dropseed is found in the same plant communities as wiregrass. In fact, it is difficult for the casual observer to distingush between these two grasses when they are not in flower. Pinewoods dropseed is a bunchgrass with densely tufted, evergreen, needlelike leaves that are relatively soft to the touch. Height of the mature blades is about 18 inches. Unlike wiregrass, pinewoods dropseed does not have a well-defined flowering season. If often responds to environmental changes like fire or unusual rains by flowering. Routine mowing may also stimulate blooms, so keep mowing to a minimum. Seed heads are an attractive reddish color on stalks about 2 feet high.

Pinewoods dropseed blends well in the wild with either wiregrass or bottlebrush three-awn. However, mixing them in a lawn is not recommended, as the three grasses produce seed heads at different times of the year. A mixed lawn would require additional mowing each time one of the grass's seed heads grew up taller than the other grasses.

Pinewoods dropseed is available from a few commercial sources, primarily as seedlings.

WILDFLOWERS TO ADD AS ACCENTS

Bunchgrasses, by their nature, do not produce the traditional carpet of lawn that we are accustomed to in suburban landscapes. Some of the "roughness," however, can be offset by adding other herbaceous plants that are compatible. Such plants should be no taller than 18 inches, capable of filling in the holes between grass clumps, not so aggressive as to replace the grass, adaptable to most lawn sites, and attractive. Several species fit these requirements in Florida.

Sunshine mimosa (*Mimosa strigillosa*) is a creeping, herbaceous plant that produces pink powderpuff flowers from spring through fall and remains green throughout the year.

Twinflower (*Dyschoriste oblongifolia*) is a creeping wildflower that produces blue flowers in late spring. It dies back each winter for several months and is not adaptable to wet sites.

Gopher apple (*Licania michauxii*) is a creeping shrub with evergreen leaves, small white flowers, and an occasional white fruit. It generally remains less than 1 foot high and prefers good drainage.

Wild petunia

Wild petunia (*Ruellia caroliniensis*) is an extremely adaptable perennial that stays less than 1 foot tall. It blooms profusely from spring through fall with lavender, petunia-like flowers that attract butterflies. Ripe seed capsules burst, dispersing seeds over a great distance, permitting the plant to establish in bare spots. Wild petunia dies back each winter for several months.

—C.H.

NATIVE LAWNS FOR

CALIFORNIA

JEANNE WIRKA & JOHN ANDERSON

HANKS TO ITS COMPLEX MOSAIC of landscape, soil, and climate types, California is blessed with a higher diversity of native plants than any other state. We enjoy a rich flora of more than 5,000 species of native vascular plants. Of these, more than 300 are grasses and many more are grasslike sedges and rushes. Until recently, however, grasses have been the least popular of the native plants commonly used for landscaping.

While native plant gardens abound in California, lawns in the state remain a monotony of non-native, water-dependent turfgrasses. Some of these exotic lawn species, such as bermudagrass (*Cynodon dactylon*), have escaped cultivation and now present a major weed problem in natural areas.

With the growing interest in native landscaping, high-maintenance monocultures are beginning to give way to stands of native grasses and sedges, many of which, once established, are drought tolerant and require much less care than traditional lawns.

Californians have a growing number of choices, as suppliers of seed and grass plugs expand the range of species available. Many new turflike varieties of native grasses and sedges are beginning to be cultivated com-

With California's growing interest in native landscaping, traditional lawns like the one in the background are beginning to give way to meadow lawns like the blue wildrye in the foreground, which is drought tolerant and requires much less care.

mercially. While all native grasses and sedges may not be available in all parts of the state, most people interested in converting their lawn to natives, with a little research, will be able to locate appropriate species (see the resources in this chapter and "Native Grass Encyclopedia" and "Nursery Sources," beginning on page 96).

Putting in a native lawn does much more than break up the monotony of traditional lawns. It is an act of conservation and restoration. Much of California's original interior was once bunchgrass prairie, dominated by perennial species such as needlegrass (*Nassella* species) and peppered with herbs and wildflowers. Blanketing the Central Valley, foothills, and central and southern coast, these grasslands once covered as much as one-fourth of the state. Over the last 150 years, they have been plowed, grazed, or converted to subdivisions; those that remain are now dominated by annual, nonnative species, many of which are noxious weeds like yellow star thistle, foxtail barley, ripgut brome, and medusahead.

NATIVE LAWN TYPES

LOW-STATURED LAWN	MEADOW LAWN
Low-growing, turflike	Taller, but can be kept tidy with mowing
More or less even surface	More or less mounding
Tends to be summer green (but depends on species)	Tends to be summer dormant (but depends on species)
Plant often has rhizomes	Mainly bunchgrasses
One or two species	Two or more species
Holds up under human traffic (a "walk-on" lawn)	Limited human traffic (a "walk-through" lawn)
	Nicely accented with perennial wildflowers

OF LAWNS AND MEADOWS

Webster's lists two definitions of lawn. The first is "an area of ground covered with grass that is kept mowed." The second, more archaic meaning is "an open space between trees." The first brings to mind kids playing ball and backyard barbecues; the second conjures up a meadow. By going native, Californians can have it either way. An easy way to distinguish between the two types: The first is a lawn to be walked *on*, the second is a lawn to be walked *through*. The general characteristics of each are shown in the box, "Native Lawn Types," above.

Considering that the vast majority of California's native grasses are taller than 12 inches when in flower, the taller meadow lawns offer many more species for creative landscaping. And even meadows can be kept tidy and lawnlike with mowing. However, mowing a native meadow or even a native grass lawn becomes less a weekly chore and more an occasional management technique to foster regrowth, flowering, or greening at key points during the year.

A regular mower, with blades set at the highest level, works fine for the lawn-type species and most of the meadow ones. Some of the densely mounding grasses, such as Idaho fescue, are easier to mow with a weed-eater (plastic blades rather than string filaments).

The striking needlegrasses, such as this purple needlegrass pictured in December, are often considered the classic California bunchgrasses.

Californians can have either a closely cropped native lawn or a meadow planting, like this one at San Francisco's Strybing Arboretum & Botanical Gardens.

ESTABLISHMENT AND MIXES

There are two ways to establish a native lawn: seeding and planting plugs. The latter is more expensive but is preferred because it gives the slower-growing native species a better chance to outcompete weeds. Furthermore, plugs provide a nearly "instant lawn," while the results of seeding may not be fully evident for a year.

Seeding rates vary widely by species but typically are in the range of 30 to 40 pounds per acre (1 pound per 1,000 square feet) when broadcast and raked in. Plug density should be about one or more plants per square foot, depending on species. Timing of seeding or planting will depend on the life cycles of the species and the climate zone. In general, cool-season grasses should be plug-planted from September to March, or seeded soon after the first rains in the fall. Warm-season species can be seeded or planted in early spring. At higher elevations the timing will be later.

The real fun in establishing a native lawn, especially a meadow-type, is developing species mixes that complement each other or mimic natural stands. For example, a lawn mix of California fescue and blue wildrye in shady sites recreates a woodland effect. A tufted hairgrass and leafy reed grass mix makes an excellent coastal lawn. To help nurse the slower-growing needlegrasses along, mix them with the faster-growing meadow barley. Larger grass species such as deergrass (*Muhlenbergia rigens*) make striking accents on the borders of either lawn type.

The most important question Californians need to ask themselves before choosing species for a native lawn is "summer green or summer dormant?" Many of California's grass species have adapted to our state's winter-wet/summer-dry climate by going dormant in the summer. Summer dormancy can be a blessing or a curse, depending on your outlook. Dormant lawns are easy to care for and require no water, but their brown color may raise an eyebrow or two. The good news is that many summer-dormant species can be kept relatively green (or at least not dead looking) through irrigation and well-timed mowing. Mixing species with slightly different life cycles can also create a sequential palette of color.

The other important factors to consider when selecting species is your climatic region and the conditions of your yard (soil, drainage, sun/shade, wet/dry). For meadow-type lawns, you may also wish to consider the "prickliness" of the species' seed heads. Consult a local nursery, botanic garden, seed supplier, or landscape architect when choosing species and mixes for your area.

NATIVE GRASSES FOR CALIFORNIA LANDSCAPES

The following lists of California native grasses include appropriate selections for both low-statured and meadow-type native lawns. We have provided site preferences when available and have given the horticultural and geographical codes listed for each species in *The Jepson Manual: Higher Plants of California* (see map on page 79). As in *The Jepson Manual*, zones in bold are especially appropriate. Consult *Jepson* for more thorough descriptions of horticultural and climate zones.

DRN: Requires excellent drainage:
IRR: Requires moderate summer watering generally one to four times per month.
SHD or **partSHD**: Does best in full or part shade; may tolerate winter or morning sun.
SUN: Does best in full sun.
WET: Roots need to be in continually wet or moist soil.

TURF-TYPE SPECIES

Agrostis pallens,
formerly *A. diegoensis*
BENTGRASS
A delicate, creeping meadow grass that spreads via rhizomes. Soft to walk on, reseeds readily. Makes a good groundcover.
DRN, partSHD: **1**, 2, 3, **4–7**, 8, 9, **14–24**

Gorgeous in summer. Not sod-forming but makes a fairly even lawn. Plant in late spring (after annual weeds die off); it will out-compete weeds the following year. Broadleaf weeding may be required in the summer. Seed densely.
DRN, SUN: **7, 15, 16**, 17
IRR: 2, 3, **8, 9, 14, 18–24**

Bouteloua gracilis
BLUE GRAMA
A warm-season bunchgrass native to California's desert region that also does well in other regions. Drought tolerant. 6 to 8 inches tall.

CAREX BREVICAULIS
A sedge that forms a dense turf. Narrow, sickle-shaped leaves grow to 6 inches tall. Mostly a coastal species, *Carex brevicaulis* likes rocky or sandy soil. Shade-tolerant. May not be as widely available as

dune sedge (*C. pansa*, below).
IRR: **4–6, 15–17**
SHD: **1–3, 7**, 8, 9, **14**, 18–24

Carex pansa
DUNE SEDGE
The hands-down winner for lawn turf (see pages 34 to 35). Fine-leafed, 4 inches tall, rhizomatous. A coastal species but does well in other regions. Very hardy; can be divided often. Prefers partial shade or full sun. Likes sandy or well-drained soil.
IRR, DRN: **4, 5, 17, 24**

Distichlis spicata
SALTGRASS
A widespread native, commonly found in salt marshes or moist alkaline areas. Summer-active, winter-dormant; grows from rhizomes. 4 to 8 inches tall. Short stems are sharp

at first but bend over to form softer turf. Can be aggressive. Only available as rhizomes or transplants.
SUN: **4–7, 14–17, 21–24**
IRR: 3, **8, 9**, 10, 11, **12, 13, 18–20**

Festuca rubra
RED FESCUE
A fine-bladed, rhizomatous fescue that can grow to be 2 feet tall, but is often mowed to 2 inches. Many varieties; 'Molate' fescue is popular for lawns. Can be kept partly green during summer with watering, but is drought-tolerant. Tolerates some shade. Not fussy about soil. Needs partial shade and irrigation in hotter parts of the state (southern California, interior valleys). Best to let it grow fairly long, then mow once in late spring.
IRR: 1, **4–6, 15–17, 24**
partSHD: 2,3,**7**,8,9,**14**, **18–23**

MEADOW-TYPE SPECIES

Calamagrostis foliosa
LEAFY REED GRASS
A coastal bunchgrass with attractive, twisted awns. *C. nutkaensis* is similar but larger. Will not do well south of San Luis Obispo. Mix with tufted hairgrass for a meadow effect.
DRN, IRR: 7, 14, 19–23
SUN: 4, **5, 15–17**, 24

Carex praegracilis
TUFTED FIELD SEDGE,
SLENDER SEDGE
Similar to dune sedge (*C. pansa*), but a more inland species. Very large range and many variants. Summer-green, bunching/rhizomatous, handles mowing well. Prefers moister sites, but drought-tolerant. Tolerates alkaline soil. Found naturally with meadow barley, saltgrass,

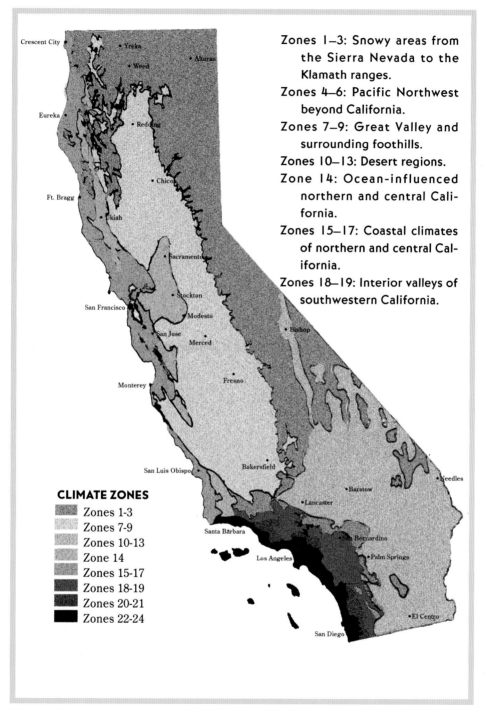

Zones 1–3: Snowy areas from the Sierra Nevada to the Klamath ranges.
Zones 4–6: Pacific Northwest beyond California.
Zones 7–9: Great Valley and surrounding foothills.
Zones 10–13: Desert regions.
Zone 14: Ocean-influenced northern and central California.
Zones 15–17: Coastal climates of northern and central California.
Zones 18–19: Interior valleys of southwestern California.

CLIMATE ZONES
Zones 1-3
Zones 7-9
Zones 10-13
Zone 14
Zones 15-17
Zones 18-19
Zones 20-21
Zones 22-24

Reprinted from *The Jepson Manual*, J. Hickman, Ed., 1993, with permission from the Jepson Herbarium. © Regents of the University of California.

and tufted hairgrass. (No horticultural codes available.)

Danthonia californica
CALIFORNIA OATGRASS
A tidy bunchgrass with attractive flowers native to coastal, coast range, and foothill areas. Mixes well with fescues for a nonprickly meadow that won't stick to your socks. With frequent mowing, can form an almost turflike groundcover and is very tolerant of foot traffic. Prefers moist and open sites.
DRN, SUN: **4–16, 15–17**
IRR: 1–3, 7, 14, **18–24**

Deschampsia caespitosa subsp. *holiciformus*
TUFTED HAIRGRASS
A lower-growing subspecies native to coastal marshes and meadows. Can be kept green with irrigation in summer. Tolerates saline water. Could make a turflike lawn if kept mowed. Mix with leafy reed grass (*Calamagrostis foliosa*).
IRR or WET, SUN: **4, 5**, 6–9, **14–17**, 18–21, **22–24**

Elymus glaucus
BLUE WILDRYE
A tall, stately bunchgrass, naturally occuring in chaparral, open areas, woodlands, and forests throughout California and the West. Less attractive than the needlegrasses, but faster growing and vigorous. Many ecotypes throughout California; coastal varieties may be smaller statured. Mow in late spring after flowering.
DRN, SUN: 4–6, 15–17
IRR: 1, **2, 3, 7**, 8, 9, **10**, 11, **14, 18–24**

Festuca californica
CALIFORNIA FESCUE
A robust woodland bunchgrass, looser and taller than Idaho fescue (*F. idahoensis*) or red fescue (*F. rubra*). Shade-tolerant. Best as a pure stand beneath deciduous trees, but try mixing with shade-tolerant native iris species for a natural effect. A variety of cultivars are available. Will survive summer drought in shady situations, but may need water in sunny locations or dry sites. Can be mowed.
4–6, IRR: **17**, 22–24
partSHD: **7**, 8, 9, **14–16**, 18–21

Festuca idahoensis
IDAHO FESCUE,
BLUE BUNCHGRASS
A densely-mounded, attractive bunchgrass with many commercially available varieties. Variety 'Mt. Tam' is most available in seed form. Goes dormant in summer but will stay green longer with occasional summer irrigtion. Mow once a year in early spring. May not do well in southern California.
DRN, IRR: 1–5, **6, 7**, 8–10, **14–24**

Hordeum brachyantherum
MEADOW BARLEY
A wet meadow bunchgrass, loose to densely tufted. Makes an excellent nurse crop in needlegrass meadows. Short-lived, but reseeds readily. Summer-dormant but thrives in winter-wet conditions. Many ecotypes are available. (No horticultural codes available.)

Leymus triticoides
CREEPING WILDRYE
A vigorous, strongly rhizomatous perennial found lining streambanks and on clay soils and bottomlands throughout California. In nature, forms dense stands that resist invasion by weeds. Stays green longer into the summer than any other cool-season perennial. Although it naturally grows quite tall, it can be mowed for a more lawnlike appearance. New varieties of lower-growing *Leymus* are also being developed for lawn use.
4, **5, 6, 15–17**
IRR: 1, **2, 3, 7–10**, 11, **14, 18–24**

Melica californica
**CALIFORNIA MELIC,
ONIONGRASS**
A delicate, partly rhizomatous grass that doesn't form dense mounds at ground level and therefore responds well to mowing. Goes dormant as early as May in hotter parts of the state. Mow after flowering. Shade-tolerant. Needs shade in southern California. Mix with needlegrasses for a grassland effect.
DRN: 2, 3, **7**, 8, 9, **14**, 18–23
SUN: 5, **15–17**, 24

Nassella pulchra
PURPLE NEEDLEGRASS

N. cernua
NODDING NEEDLEGRASS

N. lepida
FOOTHILL NEEDLEGRASS
The striking needlegrasses are often considered the classic California bunchgrasses. Hardy and drought tolerant, they do well in many environments. Full sun or partial shade. All are summer-dormant, but can be kept green with periodic mowing and monthly irrigation. Do not mow close to ground in early spring. Nodding needlegrass does best on nonclay soils. Foothill needlegrass is the smallest statured and prefers sharply drained soils. Will reseed. Many ecotypes are available.
N. cernua: DRY, SUN: **7**, 8, 9, 11, **14–24**
N. lepida: SUN or partSHD: **7**, 8, **9**, 11, **14–24**
N. pulchra: DRN, SUN: 5, **7–9**, 11, **14–24**

WILDFLOWERS TO ADD AS ACCENTS

For added color and a more natural effect in meadow lawns, try mixing in native perennial flowering plants such as blue-eyed grass (*Sisyrinchium bellum*), fleabane daisies (*Erigeron* species), goldenaster (*Heterotheca villosa*), goldenrods (*Solidago* species), hummingbird fuchsia (*Zauschneria californica*), and native irises (*Iris* species). Annual wildflowers such as lupines, poppies, tidy tips, and owl's clover can also be seeded in, but wait until the second year of establishment, to minimize competition with grass plants. —J.W. & J.A.

California fuchsia (left) and fleabane daisy (right)

CALIFORNIA NATIVE GRASS ASSOCIATION

The California Native Grass Association (CNGA) maintains a list of native grass seed vendors and growers. For more information, contact CNGA, P.O. Box 72405, Davis, California 95617-6405; (530) 759-8458.

NATIVE GRASSES FOR

HIGH DESERT LANDSCAPES

JUDITH PHILLIPS

C HOOSING THE RIGHT PLANTS is a large part of the fun and challenge of creating a beautiful garden. When selecting trees, shrubs, and flowers, we match the size, form, color, and texture of the plants with the soil, sunlight, space, and water available in the garden. Yet no matter where we garden, grass usually means lawn, and lawns have been mostly bluegrass.

Here in the Southwest, lawns have a fairly short history. Traditional gardens were walled courtyards sheltering a few cherished flowers and herbs that did double-duty as medicine or food. With the advent of sprinkler irrigation, lawns became the status quo. Until recently, at least half the water in the average household was spent in the garden, and most of that was lavished on the lawn.

As the high desert's mild climate, gorgeous scenery, and booming economy attract more and more people, our water resources are being stretched to their limits. To decrease the demand for water, gardeners are beginning to shrink their water-guzzling lawns, often replacing them with grasses that are better adapted. The network of native grasses that has quietly held the southwestern soil in place for centuries is now inching its way into gardens.

Water conservation aside, what surprises many gardeners about our native grasses is their beauty. Compared to the clipped emerald green of conventional lawns, dryland grasses are paler shades of sage green or silver blue, turning blond, tawny amber, or even rosy pink when dormant. Their limber stems and distinctive seed heads arch and nod, catching the sunlight as they dance in the breeze.

LAWN OR PRAIRIE?

Which grasses are best for your particular situation depends on the setting, how the space is used, and personal taste. The uniformity and utility of a lawn fits the bill in some situations, while the more relaxed diversity of a prairie groundcover may be more inviting in others.

Lawns are ideal surfaces to play on, and they lend a sense of continuity to the overall garden design. Of the natives, buffalograss and blue grama are similar enough in color to blend seamlessly and are fine textured and soft when maintained as a lawn.

One of the advantages of these grasses is that they are so flexible. You can mow as your schedule allows and they become more vigorous for occasionally being left to grow taller. Many a native lawn has become a soft and subtle prairie when the grass, temporarily left unclipped, begins to flower and form its eyebrowlike seedheads. When native grasses are planted as low-maintenance groundcovers for large areas, a few of the warm-season ones such as blue grama, alkali sacaton, or sideoats grama dominate, while sweeps of purple three-awn, sand bluestem, little bluestem, sand lovegrass, and deeply rooting wildflowers add contrasting color and texture.

Most of the grasses discussed in this chapter may be grown throughout the Rocky Mountain region. However, keep in mind that the temperature drops 1°F with every 100 miles northward, and 3°F with every 1,000-foot increase in elevation. Above 7,500 feet, more rain and cooler temperatures favor cool-season native grasses such as western wheatgrass, sheep fescue, and spike muhly. Other microclimate factors such as exposure and soils also influence planting options. For instance, a southwest-facing slope in Boulder, Colorado, might support blue grama, while a north-facing plain near Pueblo, Colorado, might support western wheatgrass.

GETTING NATIVE GRASSES STARTED

Even where ample moisture is available, wild stands of native grasses rarely grow as densely as a lawn. The first step toward a carpetlike native

The homeowners liked the softness of this buffalograss and blue grama so much they stopped mowing.

grass cover is soil preparation. The more water-retentive and consistent the soil, the more uniformly the grasses will cover.

First, remove the old lawn grass or clear the soil of weeds as thoroughly as possible. (See "Planting a Native Grass Lawn Step by Step," page 11.) Since southwestern soils naturally contain little organic matter, spread at least 4 inches of compost over the soil surface and till it in well. Rake the amended soil smooth and level, and water it lightly to settle the surface. Warm-season grasses such as buffalograss and blue grama need a soil temperature of at least 70°F to sprout. At 5,000-foot elevations, the soil is usually warm enough to begin seeding by May, while at elevations near 7,500 feet—about the highest elevation a warm-season native lawn will grow—the soil may not be warm enough until mid-June. Seeding should be done at least eight weeks before the first hard freeze in autumn to give the young roots time to grow deeply enough to withstand winter cold.

Another important step for native lawn success is seeding heavily enough to assure quick coverage, especially if the lawn will be used as a playfield for children and pets. Quick, dense cover also helps to minimize weed growth. Seed buffalograss and blue grama each at 2 pounds pure live seed (or PLS, a measure of the germination percentage and living dormant seed per pound), the minimum to cover 1,000 square feet of lawn. Double that rate for faster, thicker coverage. Since the chaffy seed of blue grama may be less than 50 percent PLS, it is important to know if you are purchasing bulk or PLS.

Because buffalograss seeds are much larger than fluffy blue grama, broadcast one species over the entire area as evenly as possible, then overseed with the other from the opposite direction. Rake the seed into the soil to a depth of about $1/8$ inch and roll the surface so that the seed is in firm contact with the soil. Water lightly immediately after sowing, then each morning and each evening until the thready grassblades appear. Both these grasses will germinate in five to seven days when the soil is warm and moist. Water daily until the new grass is a few inches high, then gradually begin watering less often and more deeply. Within a month you should be able to water once a week so that the water penetrates to a depth of at least 6 inches.

All-female clones of buffalograss are available as sod or plugs, and while the planting cost per square foot is much higher, sod or plugs benefit people with pollen allergies who would like to have a lawn and still be able to breathe easily. Due to cost, full-coverage sodding is usually limited to small spaces, while sod plugs may be set out 8 to 12 inches apart in a checkerboard pattern over larger areas.

When native grasses are used as prairie groundcover, they do not need to grow as uniformly or as densely as a lawn. The soil does not need to be amended with compost, but it should be tilled thoroughly so seedlings can easily root into the softened surface. The seeding rate for a prairie does not need to be quite as heavy as the rate for a lawn, but since weeds are likely to invade disturbed soil, generous seeding gives the grasses a competitive edge.

Many of the native prairie grasses are bunchgrasses growing in discrete clumps, leaving gaps for weeds to take hold. Prairie groundcover is often used to reclaim larger areas disturbed during construction, and by virtue of size alone, these seedbeds are harder to defend from marauding wildlife. Figure that a portion of seed and seedlings will feed a guestlist of quail, rabbits, voles, and ants, and add enough seed to produce a good stand of grass as well.

Once the grasses are well rooted, native lawns should be watered once a week in summer when temperatures are above 90°F, every two weeks in spring and fall, and every four to six weeks while dormant. Water should soak into the soil to a depth of 12 inches to maintain deep roots. Native grasses grown as prairie groundcover may be watered half as often, although somewhat more deeply during the growing season.

How much and when to fertilize depends on the type of grass and how much it is watered. At seeding time, bloodmeal used as a slow-release source of nitrogen may have the added advantage of repelling rabbits attracted to the new sprouts. The second year and thereafter, 1 pound of

Winecups accent a buffalograss lawn mowed occasionally to encourage growth.

nitrogen per 1,000 square feet of buffalograss and blue grama applied in April or May is enough to maintain a moderately watered lawn. Since grasses grown as prairie groundcover are watered and mowed less, they usually don't need fertilizing.

MOWING

How often and how closely to mow depends on the grasses and how they are used. Whether in a lawn or prairie, all new seedings may be mowed several times the first year to prevent fast-growing annual weeds from shading the grasses. Buffalograss planted alone or mixed with blue grama as a lawn may be mowed to a height of 3 to 4 inches as often as it grows much taller than that, typically every three to six weeks during active growth.

As a groundcover, those same grasses, once established, are shaved down to two or three inches only once a year in early spring. This mowing clears away the previous year's growth and helps to warm the soil, encouraging early regrowth. All the native grasses seem to grow more vigorously if they are never mowed shorter than 3 to 4 inches while they are actively growing, and cropped closely only in early spring as an annual cleanup. Where fire ordinances permit and plastic irrigation lines don't prevent it, large, open grass areas may be burned in early spring, imitating nature's way of revitalizing the prairie.

NATIVE GRASSES FOR HIGH DESERT LANDSCAPES

Warm-season grasses are best sown from late March through early September. Cool-season grasses are practical only at higher elevations or where groundwater is shallow. They are best sown in spring or fall when soil is cool.

The heights listed are averages; grasses receiving abundant water may grow substantially higher. The annual rainfall requirement listed is the amount the grass needs just to survive. Supplementing rainfall with deep watering once or twice a month from May through September will keep a planting attractive.

All of the seeding rates listed below are "pure live seed" (PLS), rather than bulk.

Agropyron smithii
WESTERN WHEAT
Cool-season grass growing to 30 inches. Requires at least 10 inches of annual rainfall. Seed at 3 pounds per 1,000 square feet.

Andropogon hallii
SAND BLUESTEM
Warm-season grass that grows to 30 inches. Requires at least 10 inches of annual rainfall. Seed at 1/2 pound per 1,000 square feet.

Aristida purpurea
PURPLE THREE-AWN
Warm-season grass growing to 12 inches. Requires at least 10 inches of annual rainfall. Seed at 1/2 pound per 1,000 square feet.

Bouteloua curtipendula
SIDEOATS GRAMA
Warm-season grass growing to 24 inches. Requires at least 8 inches of annual rainfall. Seed at 2 to 3 pounds per 1,000 square feet.

Bouteloua eriopoda
BLACK GRAMA
Warm-season grass that grows to 12 inches. Requires at least 6 inches of annual rainfall. Seed at 3 pounds per 1,000 square feet.

Bouteloua gracilis
BLUE GRAMA
Warm-season grass that grows to 18 inches, or 3 to 4 inches if mowed. Requires at least 10 inches of annual rainfall. For a lawn, seed at a rate of at least 4

pounds per 1,000 square ft; for a meadow, seed at 2 pounds per 1,000 square feet.

Buchloë dactyloides
BUFFALOGRASS
Warm-season grass that grows to 6 inches, or 3 to 4 inches if mowed. Requires at least 12 inches of annual rainfall. For a lawn, seed at a rate of at least 4 pounds per 1,000 square feet, for a meadow, seed at 2 to 3 pounds per 1,000 square feet.

Eragrostis trichodes
SAND LOVEGRASS
Warm-season grass grows to 30 inches. Requires at least 12 inches of annual rainfall. Seed at $1/2$ pound per 1,000 square feet.

Festuca ovina
SHEEP FESCUE
Cool-season grass that grows to 12 inches. Requires at least 10 to 14 inches of annual rainfall. Seed at 2 to 4 pounds per 1,000 square feet.

Hilaria jamesii
GALLETA
Warm-season grass that grows to 12 inches tall. Requires at least 8 inches of annual rainfall. Seed at a rate of 3 pounds per 1,000 square feet.

Muhlenbergia wrightii
SPIKE MUHLY
Cool-season grass growing to 18 inches. Requires at least 15 inches of annual rainfall. Seed at $1/4$ pound per 1,000 square feet.

Oryzopsis hymenoides
INDIAN RICEGRASS
Warm-season grass growing to 12 inches. Requires at least 6 inches of annual rainfall. Seed at 1 pound per 1,000 square feet.

Schizachyrium scoparium
LITTLE BLUESTEM
Warm-season grass grows to 18 inches. Requires at least 14 inches of annual rainfall. Seed at $1/2$ pound per 1,000 square feet.

Sporobolus airoides
ALKALI SACATON
Warm-season grass growing to 24 inches. Requires at least 8 inches of annual rainfall. Seed at $1/4$ pound per 1,000 square feet.

Sporobolus cryptandrus
SAND DROPSEED
Warm-season grass that grows to 24 inches. Requires at least 10 inches of annual rainfall. Seed at $1/4$ pound per 1,000 square feet.

WILDFLOWERS TO ADD AS ACCENTS

Wildflowers must be deeply rooted and long lived to persist in southwestern native grass prairies. The biggest challenge is finding species that won't be crowded out by the native grasses. But there are some beautiful perennials that will thrive even in the driest grasslands—those with at least 8 inches of annual rainfall—including: chocolate flower (*Berlandiera lyrata*), with its profusion of yellow daisies and chocolate aroma; bush pentemon (*Penstemon ambiguus*), with its billowy, pale pink blossoms; paperflower (*Psilostrophe tagetina*), with its small yellow flowers covering woolly white stems; desert globemallow (*Sphaeralcea ambigua*), with its pink or coral flowers; scarlet globemallow (*S. coccinea*), with its silver leaves and coral flowers; desert zinnia (*Zinnia grandiflora*), a groundcover with yellow flowers; silver-leaved golden aster (*Chrysopsis villosa*); and white-tufted evening primrose (*Oenothera caespitosa*).

For middle elevation grasslands with at least 12 inches of annual precipitation, seed in some of these wildflowers: butterflyweed (*Asclepias tuberosa*), whose pumpkin-colored flowers are a prime food source for monarch butterflies; winecups (*Callirhoe involucrata*), with its sprawling red flowers; Indian paintbrush (*Castilleja integra*), with its brilliant orange red blossoms; prairie clover (*Dalea purpurea*), with its rose pink, cloverlike flowers; gayfeather (*Liatris punctata*), featuring tall purple flower spikes; or showy goldeneye (*Viguiera multiflora*), a graceful little sunflower.   —J.P.

Indian paintbrush (left) and purple prairie clover (right)

NATIVE LAWNS FOR

COLORADO

JIM KNOPF

T hanks to recent developments in commercial buffalograss selection, there is finally a beautiful, drought-loving turf for Colorado gardeners. For larger areas, or less formal gardens, a variety of native meadow species can provide a handsome, grassy groundcover.

NEW TURF-TYPE BUFFALOGRASS

Buffalograss (*Buchloë dactyloides*), a native grass from the western Great Plains, shows extraordinary promise for widespread use as a lawn grass in hot, sunny, dry locations below 6,000 feet in Colorado. It is a warm-season grass and starts growth about a month later than turf-type tall fescue or Kentucky bluegrass, which are commonly used for Colorado lawns. Buffalograss generally goes dormant about a month earlier in the fall, as day-length shortens.

However, some of the new turf-type varieties are day-length neutral, retaining their blue-green color a month longer in the fall. Other new turf-type varieties begin spring growth several weeks earlier. It remains to be seen whether the season can be extended in both spring and fall. Winter color is an attractive, uniform tan.

Male and female flowers occur on different buffalograss plants. The male plants have attractive flowers that stand a little above the 4- to 6-inch-high leaves. Flowers on the female plants are too close to the ground to be seen from a distance. Commercial plant selection is taking advantage of this by providing all-female or mixed male and female varieties.

Because it is low growing, buffalograss does not require regular mowing, but a more traditional lawn appearance can be easily obtained by mowing every two to four weeks. Mowing often eliminates any need for chemical weed killers. In fact, it is best to control weeds by mowing, as most broadleaf herbicides damage or destroy buffalograss, often without eliminating such weeds as dandelions, bindweed, and mallow.

Water and fertilizer requirements are extremely low, too. Watering one or two times per month during the hottest Rocky Mountain weather is often all that is needed to maintain the beautiful blue-green color and discourage weeds. In fact, buffalograss needs no irrigation to survive quite well, except in the driest desert areas. This drought tolerance is creating strong interest where irrigation is not possible. Reports from Phoenix indicate the buffalograss cultivar '609' does very well when watered just once every ten days through the summer, while bermudagrass needs much more. The new female varieties of buffalograss, such as '609' and 'Prairie', are available only as sod or plugs, because seeds will produce both male and female plants.

Plugs will form a lawn, because buffalograss spreads by above-ground rooting runners. Buffalograss '609' is a widely available commercial selection that is day-length neutral, all female, and easy to establish from sod. But beware! After new sod is laid out, it nearly always goes dead-brown for a week or two before recovering. Although this is traumatic to watch, with warm weather and a little water, the grass recovers nicely.

Mixed female and male turf-type buffalograss varieties are available for seeding lawns and shortgrass meadows. Early reports about one of these mixes indicate that it "blue-greens up" earlier in the spring and holds its color later in the fall than native or earlier selections of buffalograss. However, seed varieties will probably always produce more varied lawns than sod varieties.

Buffalograss is generally not satisfactory in shade, although '609' has done well in light shade. All buffalograss types thrive in hot weather; best growth results when days are 90°F or more and nights are very warm. With so many desirable qualities, it is not surprising that buffalograss is the "hot" choice for lawns in hot, dry, sunny places.

Another unusual characteristic of buffalograss is its sexual variability. As a natural adaptation to conditions that vary enormously from year to year, some plants evolved to make the most of their precarious situation by switching sex

Buffalograss is the "hot" choice for lawns in hot, dry, sunny places.

roles. When conditions are favorable, they perform the female sex role of producing seeds. Then, when conditions are less favorable, they switch to the male sex role of producing pollen. Presumably, less favorable conditions are required to produce pollen than to produce fully developed seeds. In this way, more pollen would be produced in tough times, so that some of it can reach the few female plants that may be located in favorable but remote locations. Saltbush (*Atriplex* species) and Jack-in-the-pulpit (*Arisaema triphyllum*) are other examples of plants that have this intriguing adaptive strategy.

For the turfgrass industry, a sexually stable, female-only form of buffalograss that looked more like Kentucky bluegrass than male buffalograss, with its flowers, was considered so commercially important that techniques were developed to test the sexual stability of buffalograss selections. But the researchers were interested in more than just sexual stability. It had been observed that in nature many buffalograss varieties appeared to resist growing together, resulting in bare patches. Researchers hoped they would be able to find buffalograss selections that not only exhibited sexual stability under stress, but also the ability to form large, uniform turf areas.

Their research resulted in several successful commercial, patented, and licensed varieties of turf-type buffalograss. These are available only as sod, since seed would result in plants of both sexes and might result in other variations, too. Compared with older, seeded buffalograss selections developed for rangeland cattle forage, the new turf-types offer a new kind of uniform lawn for hot, sunny, dry situations.

NATIVE GRASS MEADOWS

There are two native Colorado meadow types—midgrass and short-grass—that are appealing to the eye and nearly self-maintaining. Residential yards, suburban open spaces, highway rights-of-way, and wildlife gardens could all benefit from using these native grass blends. They are more natural than most commercial meadow mixes and less costly to maintain than traditional, manicured lawns.

The beautiful midgrass and shortgrass meadows native to the Rocky Mountain region and Great Plains are excellent choices for sites to which each is adapted. The height of a meadow is largely determined by the species of grasses that are selected. The height should be determined not only by visual considerations but also by the meadow's intended uses. For example, it is easier to see across and walk on a shortgrass meadow than a midgrass meadow.

Shortgrass meadows tend to grow lower than ankle high and are the dominant grassland of the western high plains, where the Rocky Mountain rainshadow results in the driest conditions on the Great Plains. The dominant grasses, buffalograss and blue grama (*Bouteloua gracilis*), are best grown on very warm, dry sites. In Colorado, meadows at elevations above 6,000 feet are usually too cool and moist to remain entirely blue grama and buffalograss. They tend to evolve toward midgrass meadows.

Midgrass meadows tend to grow from knee high to waist high and are common among ponderosa pines. Boulder, Colorado, for example, has many areas of this grassland type. In many cases, these areas have been stable and attractive for 20 to 30 years with little or no maintenance.

Dominant mid-height grass species are western wheatgrass (*Agropyron smithii*), little bluestem (*Schizachyrium scoparium*), and sideoats grama (*Bouteloua curtipendula*). (Also see "Wildflowers to Add as Accents," page 95.) During dry periods in places where fire is a concern, mowing or grazing "defensible" space adjacent to buildings creates effective fire breaks. Narrow, watered lawn areas are also effective. The greatest fire danger is actually from ponderosa pines, junipers, and piñon pines that may grow in this grassland type. The grasses contain little fuel but can carry a fire to the trees and shrubs. Remove lower limbs on ponderosa pines and maintain a reasonable distance between buildings and the woody plants. Taking these precautions will usually result in a fire danger no greater than that found in a landscape with scattered trees and a watered lawn.

Meadow maintenance is largely a matter of experimentation. Watering, weeding, and mowing to mimic wildfire and browsing are the main tasks. Because Colorado shortgrass and midgrass meadows are drier than eastern meadows, invading woody shrubs and trees are rarely a problem. In fact,

Shortgrass meadows like this grassland of blue grama, blue flax, and paintbrush in Santa Fe, New Mexico, are the dominant grassland of the western high plains.

many meadows remain attractive almost indefinitely with little or no attention.

Meadows, however, are not for "neatniks" and can cause difficulty in highly groomed neighborhoods. Often the greatest maintenance challenge is surviving zealous enforcement of weed laws and quirky covenants. Fortunately, in most communities such laws are enforced on a case-by-case (or complaint-only) basis.

The way to avoid many complaints is to manage meadow edges cleverly. It's amazing how helpful a mowed strip along the edge can be, and a meadow bordered by driveways or sidewalks is usually more acceptable than a meadow that extends menacingly to a neighbor's meticulously manicured lawn.

In Colorado, many new suburban areas preserve the wonderful natural landscapes that attracted people to the area in the first place. If property values drive people to defend traditional lawnscaping, consider that Santa Fe, New Mexico, Carmel and Rancho Santa Fe, California, and the priciest neighborhoods in Boulder, Colorado, and Albuquerque, New Mexico, are all nearly lawnless.

Why use natural landscaping only in national and state parks? Office complexes, parks, homes, and roadsides would be more attractive, less costly to construct, and cheaper to maintain if natural landscaping were to replace the futile tour de force of close-cropped lawnscaping.

NATIVE GRASSES FOR COLORADO LANDSCAPES

The following selection of lower-growing native grasses is from a chart compiled by the Colorado Native Plant Society.

Agropyron dasystachyum
THICKSPIKE WHEATGRASS
Found in sandy sites at elevations of 5,000 to 10,000 feet. Height reaches 15 to 30 inches.

Danthonia parryi
PARRY OATGRASS
Found in mountains at 6,000 to 10,000 feet. Height reaches 10 to 25 inches.

Deschampsia caespitosa
TUFTED HAIRGRASS
Found in mountain meadows at elevations of 7,000 to 10,000 feet. Height reaches 30 to 50 inches.

Festuca arizonica
ARIZONA FESCUE
Found in mountains at 6,000 to 10,000 feet. Height reaches 15 to 40 inches.

Koeleria macrantha
JUNEGRASS
Found in prairies, foothills, and subalpine areas at 3,500 to 10,000 feet. Height reaches 15 to 25 inches.

Muhlenbergia cuspidata
STONEHILL MUHLY
Found in prairies and stony slopes at elevations of 5,000 to 6,000 feet. Height reaches 10 to 15 inches.

Muhlenbergia montana
MOUNTAIN MUHLY
Found in foothills and lower mountains at elevations of 5,600 to 10,000 feet. Height reaches 10 to 25 inches.

Muhlenbergia wrightii
SPIKE MUHLY
Found in plains and open slopes at elevations of 5,000 to 8,000 feet. Height reaches 10 to 25 inches.

Oryzopsis hymenoides
INDIAN RICEGRASS
Found in sandy plains and mesas at elevations of 3,500 to 9,500 feet. Height reaches 15 to 25 inches.

Poa sandbergii
SANDBERG BLUEGRASS
Found in dry plains and rocky slopes at elevations of 4,500 to 12,000 feet. Height reaches 10 to 25 inches.

Sporobolus cryptandrus
SAND DROPSEED
Found in sandy or loamy sites, at elevations of 3,500 to 8,000 feet. Height reaches 15 to 40 inches.

Sporobolus heterolepsis
PRAIRIE DROPSEED
Found in prairies and foothills at elevations of 5,000 to 7,200 feet. Height reaches 15 to 30 inches.

Stipa comata
NEEDLE-AND-THREAD
Found in plains, dry hills, and sandy sites at elevations of 3,500 to 8,500 feet. Height reaches 15 to 25 inches.

WILDFLOWERS TO ADD AS ACCENTS

Buffalograss is such a vigorous, spreading grass that it can crowd out many wildflower species. The species that compete best with buffalograss are blue flax (*Linum perenne*), purple prairieclover (*Dalea purpurea*), and stiff goldenrod (*Solidago rigida*). For best success, give wildflowers a headstart by planting them slightly before or simultaneously with buffalograss. Do not try to seed wildflowers into an established buffalograss lawn.

For shortgrass meadows dominated by blue grama, a bunchgrass that won't crowd out wildflowers, plant chocolate flower (*Berlandiera lyrata*), blanketflower (*Gaillardia aristata*), and Mexican hat coneflower (*Ratibida columnifera*).

A good example of a shortgrass meadow is at the Old Pecos Office Compound on Old Pecos Trail in Santa Fe, New Mexico. Blue grama, paintbrushes (*Castilleja* species), and blue flax were seeded under the native piñon pines. The result is a stunningly attractive, low-maintenance setting for the Santa Fe adobe-style buildings.

In midgrass meadows, purple prairieclover, pitcher or blue sage (*Salvia azurea*), and Lewis's flax (*Linum perenne* var. *lewisii*) are three wildflowers that grow well. —J.K.

Blue flax (left) and Mexican hat (right)

NATIVE GRASS ENCYCLOPEDIA

The native grasses in this list are suitable lawn substitutes. The list includes most of the grasses mentioned in the book, except those that are too tall for a lawn planting or those for which a commercial source could not be found. They all require full sun, except where otherwise noted. The numbers in the "Sources" line correspond to the suppliers and nurseries listed on pages 102 through 103.

Agrostis hyemalis
TICKLEGRASS, WINTER BENTGRASS
SITE REQUIREMENTS: Dry, moist, open forest
HEIGHT/GROWTH HABIT: 18–24"; bunching, cool season, sometimes spreads by rhizomes
TOLERATES FOOT TRAFFIC: Yes
MOWING GUIDELINES: Once a year in late winter or early spring; if mowed regularly, cut no lower than 3"
SOURCES: 8, 24 (*A. alba*, 9)

Agrostis pallens
BENTGRASS
SITE REQUIREMENTS: Meadows and woodlands
HEIGHT/GROWTH HABIT: 8–16"; bunching, cool season, sometimes rhizomatous
TOLERATES FOOT TRAFFIC: Yes
MOWING GUIDELINES: Same as *A. hyemalis*, above
SOURCE: 7

Andropogon ternarius
SPLIT-BEARD BLUESTEM, SILVER BLUESTEM
SITE REQUIREMENTS: Dry, widely adaptable; tolerates coastal conditions
HEIGHT/GROWTH HABIT: 12"; bunching, warm season
TOLERATES FOOT TRAFFIC: Yes
MOWING GUIDELINES: Once a year in late winter or early spring, no lower than 3-4"
SOURCES: 3, 11, 23

Andropogon virginicus
BROOMSEDGE, COMMON BLUESTEM
SITE REQUIREMENTS: Dry to moist, tolerates poor soil
HEIGHT/GROWTH HABIT: 12"; bunching, warm season
TOLERATES FOOT TRAFFIC: Yes
MOWING GUIDELINES: Same as *A. ternarius*, above
SOURCES: 3, 8, 9, 13, 20, 21

Aristida purpurea
PURPLE THREE-AWN
SITE REQUIREMENTS: Well-drained; drought tolerant
HEIGHT/GROWTH HABIT: 6–12"; bunching, warm season
TOLERATES FOOT TRAFFIC: Yes
MOWING GUIDELINES: Same as *A. ternarius*, above
SOURCES: 3, 16, 20, 23, 24

Aristida spiciformis
BOTTLEBRUSH THREE-AWN
SITE REQUIREMENTS: Droughty and poorly drained soils; can't take high pH.
HEIGHT/GROWTH HABIT: 10–15"; bunching, warm season
TOLERATES FOOT TRAFFIC: Yes
MOWING GUIDELINES: (Same as *A. ternarius*, above)
SOURCES: 6, 23

Aristida stricta
PINELAND THREE-AWN, WIREGRASS
SITE REQUIREMENTS: Same as *A. spiciformis*, above
HEIGHT/GROWTH HABIT: 15"; bunching, cool season
TOLERATES FOOT TRAFFIC: Yes
MOWING GUIDELINES: Same as *Andropgon ternarius*, above
SOURCES: 6 (*A. beyrichiana*, an almost identical grass in south Florida, 23)

Bouteloua curtipendula
SIDEOATS GRAMA
SITE REQUIREMENTS: Dry; drought tolerant, pH adaptable
HEIGHT/GROWTH HABIT: 12–24"; bunching, warm season
TOLERATES FOOT TRAFFIC: Yes
MOWING GUIDELINES: Could be left unmowed; if mowed, no lower than 3"
SOURCES: 1, 3, 4, 8, 9, 10, 11, 13, 16, 17, 18, 19, 20, 21, 22, 24

Bouteloua gracilis
BLUE GRAMA
SITE REQUIREMENTS: Dry; drought tolerant, can grow in sandy or loamy

soil, pH adaptable
HEIGHT/GROWTH HABIT: 8–12"; bunching, warm season
TOLERATES FOOT TRAFFIC: Yes
MOWING GUIDELINES: (Same as *B. curipendula*, above)
SOURCES: 1, 2, 3, 4, 8, 9, 10, 11, 13, 16, 17, 18, 19, 20, 21, 22, 24

Buchloë dactyloides
BUFFALOGRASS
SITE REQUIREMENTS: Dry; widely adaptable but prefers clay soil, tolerates drought, cold, and poor soil
HEIGHT/GROWTH HABIT: 4–6"; warm season, spreads by stolons
TOLERATES FOOT TRAFFIC: Yes
MOWING GUIDELINES: Not necessary, but if mowed, no lower than 3"
SOURCES: 1, 2, 4, 8, 9, 10, 11, 16, 18, 19, 20 22, 24

Carex pansa
CALIFORNIA MEADOW SEDGE, DUNE SEDGE
SITE REQUIREMENTS: Sandy or well-drained soil, coastal and inland conditions, full sun to part shade
HEIGHT/GROWTH HABIT: 4"; rhizomatous
TOLERATES FOOT TRAFFIC: Yes
MOWING GUIDELINES: Not necessary, but can mow 2–3 times a year if desired
SOURCE: 10

Carex pensylvanica
PENNSYLVANIA SEDGE, COMMON SEDGE
SITE REQUIREMENTS: Sandy soil, dappled shade
HEIGHT/GROWTH HABIT: 6–8"; creeping
TOLERATES FOOT TRAFFIC: Yes

MOWING GUIDELINES: Not necessary, but can mow 2–3 times a year to 4"
SOURCES: 8, 9, 10, 12

Carex perdentata
TEXAS MEADOW SEDGE, TEXAS HILL COUNTRY SEDGE
SITE REQUIREMENTS: Heavy or sandy soil, sun or shade
HEIGHT/GROWTH HABIT: 4–6"; creeping, almost clumping
TOLERATES FOOT TRAFFIC: Yes
MOWING GUIDELINES: Not necessary
SOURCES: 10, 14

Carex praegricilis
TUFTED FIELD SEDGE, SLENDER SEDGE
SITE REQUIREMENTS: Prefers moist sites but is drought tolerant
HEIGHT/GROWTH HABIT: 4–6"; bunching, rhizomatous
TOLERATES FOOT TRAFFIC: Yes
MOWING GUIDELINES: Not necessary, but can mow 2–3 times a year
SOURCES: : 9, 24

Carex senta
BALTIMORE SEDGE
SITE REQUIREMENTS: Deep shade, similar adaptation as *C. texensis* (below)
HEIGHT/GROWTH HABIT: 3–4"; clumping
TOLERATES FOOT TRAFFIC: Yes
MOWING GUIDELINES: Not necessary
SOURCES: 10

Carex texensis
CATLIN SEDGE
SITE REQUIREMENTS: Adapted to a wide variety of climates from Southeast to Southwest, partial to full shade

HEIGHT/GROWTH HABIT: 3–4"; clumping, matlike
TOLERATES FOOT TRAFFIC: Yes
MOWING GUIDELINES: Not necessary
SOURCES: 10

Danthonia californica
CALIFORNIA OATGRASS
SITE REQUIREMENTS: Coastal foothills; prefers moist, open sites
HEIGHT/GROWTH HABIT: 4–8"; bunching
TOLERATES FOOT TRAFFIC: Yes
MOWING GUIDELINES: Once a year in early spring
SOURCES: 5, 7, 24

Deschampsia caespitosa subsp. *holiciformus*
TUFTED HAIRGRASS
SITE REQUIREMENTS: Coastal marshes and meadows, light shade; tolerates drought
HEIGHT/GROWTH HABIT: 18–24"; bunching, cool season
TOLERATES FOOT TRAFFIC: Yes
MOWING GUIDELINES: If low height desired, mow 2–3 times a year
SOURCES: 5, 7, 10, 24

Dichanthelium species
LOW PANICUM, SWITCHGRASS
SITE REQUIREMENTS: Partial shade (like understory in open forest); tolerates varying degrees of moisture
HEIGHT/GROWTH HABIT: Three growth phases, never taller than 18"; clump that spreads, warm season
TOLERATES FOOT TRAFFIC: Yes
MOWING GUIDELINES: Not necessary, but if desired, mow only in late spring
SOURCES: 3

Distichlis spicata
SALTGRASS
SITE REQUIREMENTS: Salt marshes; moist, alkaline areas
HEIGHT/GROWTH HABIT: 8"; rhizomatous
TOLERATES FOOT TRAFFIC: Yes
MOWING GUIDELINES: If desired, mow 3–4 times per year
SOURCE: 24

Elymus glaucus
BLUE WILDRYE
SITE REQUIREMENTS: Chaparral, open areas, and woodlands
HEIGHT/GROWTH HABIT: 12–36"; bunching
TOLERATES FOOT TRAFFIC: No
MOWING GUIDELINES: Mow in late spring, after flowering
SOURCES: 5, 7, 10

Eragrostis campestris
ELLIOT'S LOVEGRASS
SITE REQUIREMENTS: : Dry, sandy soil
HEIGHT/GROWTH HABIT: 18–24"; bunching, rhizomatous, warm season
TOLERATES FOOT TRAFFIC: No
MOWING GUIDELINES: Once a year in spring
SOURCES: 6, 23

Eragrostis spectabilis
PURPLE LOVEGRASS, PETTICOAT GRASS
SITE REQUIREMENTS: Adapted to wide range of soils but not heavy, wet soil
HEIGHT/GROWTH HABIT: 12–18"; bunching with short rhizomes, warm season
TOLERATES FOOT TRAFFIC: Yes
MOWING GUIDELINES: Once a year in spring, no lower than 4"
SOURCES: 3, 4, 6, 9, 18, 20, 23

Festuca californica
CALIFORNIA FESCUE
SITE REQUIREMENTS: Woodland species; shade tolerant
HEIGHT/GROWTH HABIT: 18–24"; bunching, cool season
TOLERATES FOOT TRAFFIC: No
MOWING GUIDELINES: If desired, mow for low height, or once a year in spring
SOURCES: 5, 7, 10

Festuca idahoensis
IDAHO FESCUE, BLUE BUNCHGRASS
SITE REQUIREMENTS: Open woods, rocky slopes
HEIGHT/GROWTH HABIT: 4–8"; bunching, cool season
TOLERATES FOOT TRAFFIC: Yes
MOWING GUIDELINES: Once a year in spring
SOURCES: 5, 7, 24

Festuca ovina
SHEEP FESCUE
SITE REQUIREMENTS: Moist, well-drained; does not like hot, humid summers
HEIGHT/GROWTH HABIT: 5–10"; bunching, cool season
TOLERATES FOOT TRAFFIC: Yes
MOWING GUIDELINES: Once a year in early spring, no lower than 3"
SOURCES: 4, 5, 8, 9, 10 (many cultivars), 13, 16, 19, 22

Festuca rubra
RED FESCUE
SITE REQUIREMENTS: Widely adaptable, tolerates shade, will need some water in dry climates

HEIGHT/GROWTH HABIT: 8"; bunching, cool season
TOLERATES FOOT TRAFFIC: Yes
MOWING GUIDELINES: No lower than 3"
SOURCES: 5, 7, 8, 9, 16, 19

Festuca species
PRAIRIE NURSERY NO-MOW MIX
SITE REQUIREMENTS: : Loam, clay, and dry, sandy soils; not suited for wet soils or deep shade
HEIGHT/GROWTH HABIT: 4–6"; bunching and creeping, cool season
TOLERATES FOOT TRAFFIC: Yes
MOWING GUIDELINES: No lower than 3"
SOURCE: 17

Hilaria jamesii
GALLETA
SITE REQUIREMENTS: Well-drained, sandy soil
HEIGHT/GROWTH HABIT: 12–20"; rhizomatous, warm season
TOLERATES FOOT TRAFFIC: Yes
MOWING GUIDELINES: Once a year in early spring, no lower than 3"
SOURCES: 16, 24

Hordeum brachyantherum
MEADOW BARLEY
SITE REQUIREMENTS: Moist site, bottomlands
HEIGHT/GROWTH HABIT: 8–30"; bunching, cool season
TOLERATES FOOT TRAFFIC: No
MOWING GUIDELINES: Once a year in early spring
SOURCES: 5, 7, 24

Koeleria macrantha (K. cristata)
JUNEGRASS
SITE REQUIREMENTS: Dry, gravelly, drought tolerant
HEIGHT/GROWTH HABIT: 16–20"; bunching, cool season
TOLERATES FOOT TRAFFIC: Yes
MOWING GUIDELINES: Mow no lower than 3"
SOURCES: 3, 5, 8, 9, 11, 17, 18, 20, 24

Melica californica
CALIFORNIA MELIC, ONIONGRASS
SITE REQUIREMENTS: Mountain meadows, rocky woods; shade tolerant, needs shade in southern California
HEIGHT/GROWTH HABIT: 2' to 4'; does not mound at ground level, cool season
TOLERATES FOOT TRAFFIC: No
MOWING GUIDELINES: Once a year after flowering
SOURCE: 7

Muhlenbergia capillaris
PURPLE MUHLY, MUHLY GRASS
SITE REQUIREMENTS: Sandy or rocky soil; tolerates drought and wind
HEIGHT/GROWTH HABIT: 12"; bunching, warm season
TOLERATES FOOT TRAFFIC: No
MOWING GUIDELINES: Once a year in early spring, no lower than 3"
SOURCES: 3, 6, 15, 23

Muhlenbergia wrightii
SPIKE MUHLY
SITE REQUIREMENTS: High elevations in West where more rainfall occurs
HEIGHT/GROWTH HABIT: bunching, cool season
TOLERATES FOOT TRAFFIC: No

MOWING GUIDELINES: Once year in spring, no lower than 3"
SOURCES: 24

Nassella cernua
NODDING NEEDLEGRASS
SITE REQUIREMENTS: Foothills
HEIGHT/GROWTH HABIT: 1–2'; bunching, cool season
TOLERATES FOOT TRAFFIC: Yes, if mowed
MOWING GUIDELINES: Mow 2–3 times a year; do not mow close to ground in early spring
SOURCE: 7

Nassella lepida
FOOTHILL NEEDLEGRASS
SITE REQUIREMENTS: Dry hills, open woods, rocky slopes
HEIGHT/GROWTH HABIT: 1–2'; bunching, cool season
TOLERATES FOOT TRAFFIC: Yes, if mowed
MOWING GUIDELINES: Same as *N. cernua,* above
SOURCES: 5, 7

Nassella pulchra
PURPLE NEEDLEGRASS
SITE REQUIREMENTS: Widely adaptable, drought tolerant; full sun to part shade
HEIGHT/GROWTH HABIT: 1–2'; bunching, cool season
TOLERATES FOOT TRAFFIC: Yes, if mowed
MOWING GUIDELINES: Same as *N. cernua,* above
SOURCES: 5, 7, 10

Oplismenus setarius
BASKETGRASS, WOODSGRASS
SITE REQUIREMENTS: Moist shade
HEIGHT/GROWTH HABIT: 3"; creeping, forms roots on the stem where it touches soil surface
TOLERATES FOOT TRAFFIC: Yes, but only light traffic
MOWING GUIDELINES: Not necessary
SOURCE: 23

Oryzopsis hymenoides
INDIAN RICEGRASS
SITE REQUIREMENTS: Well-drained, sandy soil; tolerates heavy soil and alkaline conditions, drought tolerant
HEIGHT/GROWTH HABIT: 12–14"; bunching, cool season
TOLERATES FOOT TRAFFIC: No
MOWING GUIDELINES: Once a year in early spring
SOURCES: 3, 16, 19, 24

Schizachyrium scoparium
LITTLE BLUESTEM
SITE REQUIREMENTS: Dry to moist; pH adaptable
HEIGHT/GROWTH HABIT: 12–24"; bunching, warm season
TOLERATES FOOT TRAFFIC: Yes
MOWING GUIDELINES: Once a year in early spring
SOURCES: 1, 3, 4, 8, 9, 10, 13, 16, 17, 18, 19, 20, 21, 22, 23, 24

Sporobolus junceus
PINEWOODS DROPSEED
SITE REQUIREMENTS: Droughty soils of upland pinelands and poorly drained soil of Florida prairies
HEIGHT/GROWTH HABIT: 18"; bunching, warm season
TOLERATES FOOT TRAFFIC: Yes
MOWING GUIDELINES: Once a year in early spring
SOURCES: 6, 23

NURSERY SOURCES

When shopping for native grasses try to obtain seed from a source as close to your location as possible. Some species occur across a wide geographic range, but local ecotypes are better adapted to the specific site where they are found. If this list does not provide a source close to where you live, contact your county Extension Service, native plant society (a list is available at the Wild Ones Web site: www.for-wild.org), or Audubon Society.

1 Allendan Seed
1966 175th Lane
Winterset, IA 50273
(515) 462-1241
Fax (515) 462-4084

2 Arkansas Valley Seed Co.
4625 Colorado Blvd.
P.O. Box 16025
Denver, CO 80216
(303) 320-7500

3 Bluestem Nursery
4101 Curry Road
Arlington, TX 76001
(817) 478-6202
Email: grassman@flash.net

4 Browning Seed, Inc.
P.O. Box 1836
Plainview, TX 79073-1836
(800) 243-5271
Fax (806) 293-9050
www.browningseed.com

5 Central Coast Wilds
114 Liberty St.
Santa Cruz, CA 95060
(408) 459-0656
www.centralcoastwilds.com

6 Central Florida Native Flora, Inc.
P.O. Box 1045
33601 Kiefer Road
San Antonio, FL 33576-1045
(352) 588-3687
Fax (352) 588-4552

7 Elkhorn Native Plant Nursery
P.O. Box 270
Moss Landing, CA 95039
(831) 763-1207
Fax (831) 763-1659

8 Ernst Conservation Seeds
9006 Mercer Pike
Meadville, PA 16335
(800) 873-3321
Fax (814) 336-5191
www.ernstseed.com
$25 minimum order

9 Genesis Nursery
23200 Hurd Road
Tampico, IL 61283
(815) 438-2220
Fax (815) 438-2222

10 Greenlee Nursery
257 E. Franklin Ave.
Pomona, CA 91766
(909) 629-9045

11 Hamilton Seeds
16786 Brown Road
Elk Creek, MO 65464
(417) 967-2190

12 Ion Exchange
Native Seed and Plant Nursery
1878 Old Mission Drive
Harpers Ferry, IA 52146
(800) 291-2143
Fax (319) 535-7362
www.ionxchange.com

13 Limerock Ornamental Grasses
70 Sawmill Road
Port Matilda, PA 16870
(814) 692-2272

14 McNeal Growers
P.O. Box 371
Manchaca, TX 78652

15 Plant Delights Nursery
9241 Sauls Road
Raleigh, NC 27603-9326
(919) 772-4794
Fax (919) 662-0370
www.plantdel.com

16 Plants of the Southwest
Agua Fria Rd., Rt. 6, Box 11-A
Santa Fe, NM 87501
(800) 788-7333
Fax (505) 438-8800
www.plantsofthesouthwest.com

17 Prairie Nursery
P.O. Box 306
Westfield, WI 53964
(800) 476-9453
Fax (608) 296-2741
www.prairienursery.com

18 Prairie Moon Nursery
Rt. 3 Box 163
Winona, MN 55987-9515
(507) 452-1362
Fax (507) 454-5238
www.prairiemoonnursery.com

19 Rocky Mountain Seed Co.
1325 15th St.
P.O. Box 5204
Denver, CO 80217
(303) 623-6223

20 Sharp Brothers Seed Co.
396 S.W. Davis St.
Clinton, MO 64735
(660) 885-7551

21 Shooting Star Nursery
444 Bates Road
Frankfort, KY 40601
(502) 223-1679
Email: shootsn@aol.com

22 Stock Seed Farms, Inc.
28008 Mill Road
Murdock, NE 68407-2350
(800) 759-1520
Fax (402) 867-2442
www.stockseed.com

23 The Natives
2929 JB Carter Road
Davenport, FL 33837
(941) 422-6664
Fax (941) 421-6520

24 Western Native Seed
P.O. Box 1463
Salida, CO 81201
(719) 539-1071
Fax (719) 539-6755
castle.chaffee.net/~westseed

CONTRIBUTORS

WILL CORLEY recently retired as Wildflower Project Coordinator at the University of Georgia Griffin Experiment Station. In the early 1980s, he evaluated hundreds of grasses for possible ornamental use, rejecting all but 12. He is now affiliated with S&S Environmental Landscape Consultants in Griffin, Georgia.

STEVIE DANIELS is the director of publications for Lafayette College in Easton, Pennsylvania. She is the the author of *The Wild Lawn Handbook: Alternatives to the Traditional Front Lawn* (Macmillan, 1995) and gardening columnist for *Pennsylvania Magazine*. She has been a Penn State Master Gardener since 1988. Daniels has spent the last three years replacing the grass in her own yard with native plants and a front lawn of native grasses.

JOHN GREENLEE, dubbed "The Grassman" by Wade Graham of *The New Yorker*, established Greenlee Nursery in 1985 and is the author of *The Encyclopedia of Ornamental Grasses* (Rodale Press, 1992).

JAMES C. GRIMES is the owner of Fort Pond Native Plants in Montauk, Long Island, New York.

CRAIG HUEGEL, an urban wildlife specialist and expert on native Florida plants for use in home landscapes, is director of the Brooker Creek Preserve, north of Tampa, Florida.

JIM KNOPF is a landscape architect with a yard full of native plants, wildlife, and a small buffalograss lawn in Boulder, Colorado. He is the author of *The Xeriscape Flower Gardener: A Waterwise Guide for the Rocky Mountain Region*, and is completing a companion book, *Waterwise Landscaping with Trees, Shrubs, and Vines: A Xeriscape Guide for the Rocky Mountain Region, California, and the Desert Southwest.*

WILLIAM A. NIERING is research director of the Connecticut Arboretum and a professor of botany at Connecticut College. He is also the editor of the journal *Restoration Ecology*.

JUDITH PHILLIPS is a landscape designer and owner of Bernardo Beach Native Plant Farm, in Veguita, New Mexico. The author of

Southwestern Landscaping with Native Plants, she has been growing and using native grasses in her designs for more than 15 years.

TERRANCE P. RIORDAN is a professor of horticulture at the University of Nebraska, where he teaches a graduate course in turfgrass management. He received his Ph.D. in agronomy from Purdue University in 1970. In 1997, he received the Fred V. Grau Turfgrass Science Award. His work with buffalograss for the past 15 years has led to the release of eight improved turf-type cultivars.

JEANNE WIRKA, currently pursuing a doctorate in restoration ecology, is managing a riparian restoration project in Winters, California, using many of the species mentioned in the chapter on native grasses for California. She is editor of *Grasslands*, the quarterly newsletter of the California Native Grass Association (CNGA).

JOHN ANDERSON, owner of Hedgerow Farms—where all of the species mentioned in this chapter are grown—and board member of CNGA, is a habitat restorationist and ecosystem manager. They thank David Amme, John Greenlee, Ron Lutsko, and Scott Stewart for information that contributed to this chapter.

ILLUSTRATIONS

BOBBI ANGELL
pages 17, 27, 33, 37, 43
RICHARD L. BITNER
pages 1, 47, 49 (left & right), 57
STEVE BUCHANAN
pages 12 through 15
DAVID CAVAGNARO
pages 7, 9, 10, 30, 40 (top & bottom), 58 (top), 68, 80 (left), 88 (right), 95 (right)
WILL CORLEY
page 61
NEIL DIBOLL,
PRAIRIE NURSERY
page 29

JOHN GREENLEE
page 35
JAMES C. GRIMES
page 45 (top & bottom), 51, and 52 (top & bottom)
CRAIG HUEGEL
page 65
JIM KNOPF
page 93
RON LUTSKO
page 73 (bottom)
WILLIAM A. NIERING,
page 55
WILLIAM MEYER
page 39

JERRY PAVIA pages 58 (bottom), 62 (bottom), 88 (left), 95 (left)
JUDITH PHILLIPS
pages 83 and 85
TERRANCE P. RIORDAN
page 23
SANDY SNYDER
page 21
ANDY WASOWSKI
cover, pages 5, 19, 25, 62 (top), 80 (right), 91
JEANNE WIRKA
pages 71 and 73 (top)

BROOKLYN BOTANIC GARDEN

MORE

BOOKS ON

NATIVE LAWNS &

NATURAL

GARDENING

31901051702738